What others are saying about this book:

"What a timely piece! Just what we in several of my new task forces and working groups have been looking for to accomplish one of the chief goals of my new administration - to enhance and encourage civic education in Connecticut. There is indeed a crisis in civics…"

Denise Merrill
Connecticut Secretary of State

"After reading this book, I am confident that you will once again share in that same pride and appreciation for the greatness that is America and will be better able to play a role in keeping it that way."

Trey Grayson
Director, Institute of Politics
Harvard University
Kentucky Secretary of State (2004-2011)

"America has been blessed with a rich heritage and the finest Constitution ever written. Unfortunately too many Americans have not been taught adequately about these subjects. This book is an excellent resource for every American citizen."

Kris W. Kobach
Kansas Secretary of State
Professor of Constitutional Law
University of Missouri – Kansas City 1996-2010

"*CITIZENSHIP* should serve as a wake up call. We live in the greatest nation on earth, founded on personal rights and responsibilities, yet we fail to teach our citizens of all ages the history that made America what it is today. This book is a good start."

Max Maxfield
Wyoming Secretary of State

"An immediate, dramatic turnaround is required of American citizens. Fortunately, StarGroup has recognized this by publishing this most timely, greatly needed, very patriotic book. It tells its readers about the vision and contributions of our Founding Fathers, what America really is, why we are fortunate to be an American and should love it dearly, and how we, ourselves, can help make it the great nation it has been. This is a must read for all good citizens."

Brigadier General Albin F. Irzyk USA,
Veteran WWII, VN, Cold War

"This book is a powerful hands-on, interactive experience. Pick it up and you'll get into it—testing yourself on citizenship, filling in the gaps on the American platform and appreciating the many personal wonders provided by not only our Founding Fathers, but today's citizens who love this country. You'll want to jump in and be more proactive about citizenship as part of your world."

Roger Klietz
President—Living Arts College

"This book is a must for every family, including the Holtz family. We have an obligation to tell our children what made this country great, as the schools now fail to do so."

Lou Holtz
Football Coach
College Football Hall of Fame Class of 2008

"*CITIZENSHIP* encourages readers to learn about and participate in civic life. It simultaneously educates and inspires, eloquently urging every American to partake in a more active citizenry."

David B. Smith
Executive Director
National Conference on Citizenship

"*CITIZENSHIP* is a superb primer for all Americans. It is Civics 101, the basics that every citizen and patriot should know about our magnificent country. Brenda Star has done a truly great service in compiling this important work."

General Anthony C. Zinni
USMC (Retired)

"Business people like being prepared. We like having our facts ready and knowing our industry well, but how many of us can say the same for our knowledge of the Constitution or how our country works? This book is the perfect guide to the principles that govern so many parts of our lives, in and out of business. Being without it means not being prepared and not knowing some of the basic items that all of us should be proud of. It should be a must read and on every bookshelf."

Dean A. Deyo
President Emeritus - Time Warner
Communications
President - Memphis Music Foundation

"This book is a concise, entertaining, educational and enlightening work that will both inform and ignite the passion in every American. What sets this work apart from all other citizen guides is the invitation to make a difference through active participation, volunteerism and heartfelt compassion for our military including war veterans, disaster survivors, seniors and the disabled. We are all one America. Whatever path we travel, we do not walk alone."

Stephanie Haridopolos, M.D.
First Lady of the Florida Senate 2010-2012

"*CITIZENSHIP* is a must read for everyone from children to grandparents to ensure every American knows the basic history of our great country and how our government works. This book is an essential tool for preparing active and engaged citizens to carry our proud history forward."

Rich DeVos
Founder of Amway and Chairman
of the Orlando Magic

An extremely well researched and fact-based book. As a naturalized citizen of this great country, I only wish that Brenda Star had been there earlier to help enlighten our historic and civic knowledge. This is a wonderful overview.

Dr. Eduardo Prado Ayau
International Dental Arts

"The information in this book is vital and well presented. I love it!"

Adam Clatsoff, President
ADCAHB

"The United States is losing the bridge between our heritage and our future. *CITIZENSHIP* is the repair kit. Pray that it works."

Sid Dinerstein
Author of Adults Only - For Those Who Love
Their Country More Than Their Party"

"Let's acknowledge this: the United States, whatever its faults, is an exceptional and exalted nation - still a beacon to the world. Our challenge is to keep it that way and to embrace it.

The reshaping of the United States is underway, and this book, rooted in the basics, is a blueprint for all who intend to be in the process."

Robert Dilenschneider
Chairman & Founder
The Dilenschneider Group

"This book really does contain important information that every American needs to know. Congratulations on a job well done!"

Vince Naimoli
Chairman Emeritus/Founder
Tampa Bay Rays

"This book has great information about American history. It was fun to read. I shared a lot of information with my parents and friends. Now I know how to say the 'Pledge of Allegiance.'"

Rohith Karthic
Age 5
Kindergartener
Author of Hey Kids, America Needs Us!

"Every U.S. citizen should keep this book handy. It is chock-full of information we all should know. Kudos to Brenda Star for recognizing the serious need for this book."

John C. Randolph
Chairman
Palm Beach Fellowship of Christians and Jews

"Americans need thoughtful and effective civic education now more than ever, and the Center for Civic Education's national network welcomes all contributions to the common enterprise of education for democracy. *CITIZENSHIP* includes many interesting items, such as the inspirational stories that might catch the eye of readers and interest them in the ideals of "Exactly what America needs at exactly the right time! We can never take for granted the privilege of being an American. This book not only challenges your knowledge of America, but it challenges you to be a better American."

Nasser Kazeminy
Chairman, National Ethnic Coalition of
Organizations Foundations, Inc.

"In reviewing the many writings in this excellent book, we are reminded that words indeed matter. Through *CITIZENSHIP* we see that the values which have distinguished the United States, such as liberty, equal justice for all, and the rule of law, are compelling and enduring."

Scott Gardner Hawkins, Esquire
President, The Florida Bar (2011-2012)

"Brenda Star is a genius. No other subject is more timely nor important during this critical time in our American history than understanding and truly appreciating the unique heritage we are privileged to enjoy. This very concise and readable book should be in every household and schoolroom in America for study and reference. We will survive with an educated AND responsible citizenry. Brenda Star's wonderful book reminds us again of these responsibilities."

Jon K. Thompson
West Point Graduate
Vietnam Veteran
Former Board member of the National Defense
University Foundation
Past President and Chairman of the Defense
Orientation Conference Association

"*CITIZENSHIP* includes many interesting items. It could be useful to Americans young and old"

John H. Hale
Associate Director
Center for Civic Education

Other Books
by StarGroup International

Hey Kids, America Needs Us!
(First Edition 2011)

101 Reasons to READ With Your Child
(First Edition 2000)
(Second Edition 2002)
(Third Edition 2009)
(Fourth Edition 2011)
(Fifth Edition 2012)

101 Reasons to Be a Proud American
(2001)

Celebrating AMERICA
(2004)

The History of The DEMOCRATIC Party
(2004)

The History of The REPUBLICAN Party
(2004)

CITIZENSHIP

WHAT
EVERY
AMERICAN
NEEDS
TO KNOW

COMPILED BY
BRENDA STAR

STAR
GROUP

BOOKS

StarGroup International, Inc. West Palm Beach, Florida

Concept & supervision by Brenda Star

Book design by Mel Abfier
Cover design by Roger Klietz and Mel Abfier
Senior Editor: Shawn McAllister
Research/Writers: Shawn McAllister, Cheryl Kravetz, Gary Edelson, Susan Stallone

Contributing Editors:
Laurel Baker, Gwen Carden, Sandra Thompson, Jane Evers, Patti Sans, Tommi Pardu, Terry van Rhyn, Rosilu Cuevas, Jeff Lawlor, Steve L. Seftenberg

Designed and produced by StarGroup International, Inc.
(561) 547-0667
www.stargroupinternational.com

Printed in the United States of America

Library of Congress Cataloging-in-Publication Data pending.

CITIZENSHIP - What Every American Needs To Know
ISBN 978-1-884886-60-7

Book Orders
• Bulk/customized book orders: www.stargroupinternational.com

• Single book orders: www.amazon.com

• Sponsorships for distribution can be made through
StarGroup International
1194 Old Dixie Highway, Suite 201
West Palm Beach, Florida 33403

561-547-0667
info@stargroupinternational.com

SPECIAL THANKS

To Jay Leno for his "man on the street" interviews that made me want to laugh at the answers and cry at the reality at the same time.

To Stephen Zack (Past President of the American Bar Association) who, when showcased in a feature article in Florida Trend magazine, discussed his concern for waning civics education in many public schools. His commitment to make a difference inspired me to accept the challenge and join the cause.

And, to the friends, family and staff whose thoughts, ideas and hard work made this book a reality.

TABLE OF CONTENTS

INTRODUCTION

Recent media reports about Americans having a severe lack of knowledge about our country and its history is a haunting reality. There was a time when people around the world recognized the U.S. as a world leader. We felt proud, safe and secure. That's not the case today.

What is this *test* that we Americans can't pass? What is this information that we don't know? Could this lack of knowledge be part of what is affecting our economy, our world leadership, our ability to make intelligent decisions as voters? I found the focus of the tests to be on important events and documents that have been the foundation of our country and the structure of our judicial system. This compiled information will help us become more aware of American government and history, and our responsibility as American citizens.

America is at a turning point. How can we recapture the strength and influence that once uniquely belonged to us? How do we energize our citizens to take responsibility for the future? We must do something. The next generation is counting on us.

First, we must educate ourselves – A high percentage of American citizens do not know enough about American history or government.

• In February of 2011, *Newsweek* gave 1,000 Americans the U.S. Citizenship Test and 38% failed.

• Only 24% of high school seniors were "proficient" in the subject and only 4% were "advanced," based on The National Assessment of Educational Progress (NAEP) Civics Assessment of 2010.

• Only 51% of respondents feel able to understand politics and government, according to the 2008 Civic Health Index.

In May of 2011, *The New York Times* reported the National Assessment of Educational Progress (NAEP) results for 2010:

• Fewer than half of American eighth graders knew the purpose of the Bill of Rights.

• Three-quarters of high school seniors who took the NAEP were unable to demonstrate civic skills such as identifying the effect of United States foreign policy on other nations or naming a power granted to Congress by the Constitution.

Second, we must boost pride in our country.

• Only one in three Americans (32%) say they are "extremely patriotic," according to a 2010 USA Today/Gallup poll.

• 14% of respondents were not "proud to be American" in a 2009 Pew Research Center poll.

• Only 23% of respondents in the 2008 Civic Health Index think that government in Washington generally does what is right.

Third, we must inspire civic engagement.

• Only 36% of adults are part of a political or civic group, according to a recent Pew Internet poll.

• 47.8% voted nationally in the 2010 midterm elections.

• While 67% of respondents said that volunteering was personally important to them, the 2008 Civic Health Survey revealed that only 27% actually do volunteer.

The United States and our history are worth knowing.

Respect your nation; know your country.

PREFACE

What follows in this book is a treasure trove of information about the United States, its history, and its proud traditions. It lays out all of the elements of what it takes to become a good citizen. But why is being a good citizen so important?

A country filled with good citizens runs smoothly because its people stay informed about the issues, vote for the best candidates, obey laws, serve on juries, volunteer time to others, and care about education. A country filled with good citizens is stronger, safer, and has more global influence. All of us want a country filled with good citizens – and it is incumbent upon each of us to make it happen.

To build citizenship, a good start is to read this book. Even the most active, involved, patriotic individuals will find something in this book they didn't know. A second step is to follow the suggestions at the end of this book about how to be a better American citizen. Volunteer, participate in a civic group, and find new ways to build connections and make your community stronger.

Last but not least, help a young person. Studies show that people who have college degrees have higher rates of voting, volunteering, and community participation. Yet far too many students are not on a track to go to college or even know what it takes to go to college. And sadly, many of our country's public schools don't have the resources or services to help kids get to where they need to go. Step up, reach out, and help a student find his or her way to a brighter future. The young people we help today will become the active, engaged, proud American citizens of the future.

Charles B. Reed
Chancellor, California State University

FOREWORD

What does it mean to be a United States citizen? What binds us together as Americans? It is easy to go through our daily lives without stopping to consider these questions.

As you explore CITIZENSHIP: *What Every American Needs to Know*, I encourage you to think about how citizenship plays a role in your life and that of your family, friends, neighbors, and fellow Americans. I hope you will take time to reflect on our constitutional democracy and its fundamental principles and values, including the rule of law, separation of powers, an independent and impartial judiciary and the protection of individual freedoms.

What ties us uniquely together as Americans is not place or even bonds of blood but a commitment to shared ideals of political community. The cornerstone of these ideals and of our republican system of government is the United States Constitution. That historic document, originally drafted in 1787, established the blueprint of government still in place today. The Constitution organized the federal government to include three co-equal branches: the legislative, the executive and the judicial. Placing checks and balances upon these branches of government prevents any one of them from holding and exercising too much power.

This system enables us to participate in our own government, whether directly or through our elected representatives. Being an engaged and active citizen starts locally: serving on juries, voting, communicating with elected officials, following current events and volunteering in the community.

In order to be engaged citizens, however, all of us have the responsibility to be informed citizens. As James Madison, the "father of the Constitution," observed, "Knowledge will forever govern ignorance; and a people who mean to be their own governors must arm themselves with the power which knowledge gives." Why is knowledge so important for citizens? Madison emphasized, "The advancement and diffusion of knowledge is the only guardian of true liberty."

Educating ourselves as citizens is central to the success of our constitutional democracy. It means appreciating our common law history as a people and the special role that courts play as guardians of the Constitution. It means recognizing the responsibilities as well as the rights of citizenship.

As individual citizens, we all have a duty to help our nation live up to the ideal articulated memorably by Abraham Lincoln in the Gettysburg Address: "government of the people, by the people, for the people."

Wm. T. (Bill) Robinson III

President-Elect (2010-11)
American Bar Association
Attorney At Law
Frost Brown Todd LLC

CIVICS TESTS

Test your knowledge of our nation's founding principles

Intercollegiate Studies Institute Full Civic Literacy Exam

The Intercollegiate Studies Institute (ISI), a non-profit, non-partisan, educational organization that works "to educate for liberty," seeks to enhance the rising generation's knowledge of our nation's founding principles – limited government, individual liberty, personal responsibility, the rule of law, market economy and moral norms. The ISI recently administered an exam where the average score for all 2,508 Americans taking the test was 49%; college educators scored 55%.

To find out how you fare in relation to those test scores, you can take the same exam administered by the ISI found on the following pages.

Want to find out how you would do on the U.S. Naturalization test? Check out Chapter 2.

1. Which of the following are the unalienable rights referred to in the Declaration of Independence?

    a. life, liberty, and property
    b. honor, liberty, and peace
    c. liberty, health, and community
    d. life, respect, and equal protection
    e. life, liberty, and the pursuit of happiness

2. In 1933 Franklin Delano Roosevelt proposed a series of government programs that became known as:

    a. the Great Society
    b. the Square Deal
    c. the New Deal
    d. the New Frontier
    e. supply-side economics

3. What are the three branches of government?

    a. executive, legislative, judicial
    b. executive, legislative, military
    c. bureaucratic, military, industry
    d. federal, state, local

4. What was the main issue in the debates between Abraham Lincoln and Stephen A. Douglas in 1858?

    a. is slavery morally wrong?
    b. would slavery be allowed to expand to new territories?
    c. do Southern states have the constitutional right to leave the union?
    d. are free African Americans citizens of the United States?

5. The United States Electoral College:

    a. trains those aspiring for higher political office
    b. was established to supervise the first televised presidential debates

    c. is otherwise known as the U.S. Congress

    d. is a constitutionally mandated assembly that elects the President

    e. was ruled undemocratic by the Supreme Court

6. The Bill of Rights explicitly prohibits:

    a. prayer in public school

    b. discrimination based on race, sex, or religion

    c. the ownership of guns by private individuals

    d. establishing an official religion for the United States

    e. the President from vetoing a line item in a spending bill

7. What was the source of the following phrase: "Government of the people, by the people, for the people"?

    a. the speech "I Have a Dream"

    b. Declaration of Independence

    c. U.S. Constitution

    d. Gettysburg Address

8. In 1935 and 1936 the Supreme Court declared that important parts of the New Deal were unconstitutional. President Roosevelt responded by threatening to:

    a. impeach several Supreme Court justices

    b. eliminate the Supreme Court

    c. appoint additional Supreme Court justices who shared his views

    e. override the Supreme Court's decisions by gaining three-quarter majorities in both houses of Congress

9. Under our Constitution, some powers belong exclusively to the federal government. What is one power of the federal government?

    a. make treaties

    b. make zoning laws

    c. maintain prisons

    d. establish standards for doctors and lawyers

10. Name one right or freedom guaranteed by the First Amendment.

    a. right to bear arms
    b. right to due process
    c. freedom of religion
    d. right to counsel

11. What impact did the Anti-Federalists have on the United States Constitution?

    a. their arguments helped lead to the adoption of the Bill of Rights
    b. their arguments helped lead to the abolition of the slave trade
    c. their influence ensured that the federal government would maintain a standing army
    d. their influence ensured that the federal government would have the power to tax

12. Which of the following statements is true about abortion?

    a. it was legal in most states in the 1960s
    b. the Supreme Court struck down most legal restrictions on it in *Roe v. Wade*
    c. the Supreme Court ruled in *Plessy v. Ferguson* that underage women must notify their parents of an impending abortion
    d. the National Organization for Women has lobbied for legal restrictions on it
    e. it is currently legal only in cases of rape or incest, or to protect the life of the mother

13. Socrates, Plato, Aristotle, and Aquinas would concur that:

    a. all moral and political truth is relative to one's time and place
    b. moral ideas are best explained as material accidents or byproducts of evolution

     c. values originating in one's conscience cannot be judged by others

     d. Christianity is the only true religion and should rule the state

     e. certain permanent moral and political truths are accessible to human reason

14. The Puritans:

     a. opposed all wars on moral grounds

     b. stressed the sinfulness of all humanity

     c. believed in complete religious freedom

     d. colonized Utah under the leadership of Brigham Young

     e. were Catholic missionaries escaping religious persecution

15. The phrase that in America there should be a "wall of separation" between church and state appears in:

     a. George Washington's Farewell Address

     b. the Mayflower Compact

     c. the Constitution

     d. the Declaration of Independence

     e. Thomas Jefferson's letters

16. In his "I Have a Dream" speech, Dr. Martin Luther King, Jr.:

     a. argued for the abolition of slavery

     b. advocated black separatism

     c. morally defended affirmative action

     d. expressed his hopes for racial justice and brotherhood

     e. proposed that several of America's founding ideas were discriminatory

17. Sputnik was the name given to the first:

     a. telecommunications system

     b. animal to travel to space

c. hydrogen bomb

d. manmade satellite

18. Susan B. Anthony was a leader of the movement to:

a. guarantee women the right to vote in national elections

b. guarantee former slaves the right to vote

c. ensure that harsher laws against criminals were passed

d. reduce the authority of the Constitution of the United States

19. The Scopes "Monkey Trial" was about:

a. freedom of the press

b. teaching evolution in the schools

c. prayer in the schools

d. education in private schools

20. Who is the commander in chief of the U.S. military?

a. Secretary of the Army

b. Secretary of State

c. President

d. Chairman of the Joint Chiefs of Staff

21. Name two countries that were our enemies during World War II.

a. Canada and Mexico

b. Germany and Japan

c. England and Spain

d. China and Russia

22. What part of the government has the power to declare war?

a. Congress

b. the President

c. the Supreme Court

d. the Joint Chiefs of Staff

23. In October 1962 the United States and the Soviet Union came close to war over the issue of Soviet:

    a. control of East Berlin
    b. missiles in Cuba
    c. support of the Ho Chi Minh regime in Viet Nam
    d. military support of the Marxist regime in Afghanistan

24. In the area of United States foreign policy, Congress shares power with the:

    a. President
    b. Supreme Court
    c. state governments
    d. United Nations

25. Free enterprise or capitalism exists insofar as:

    a. experts managing the nation's commerce are appointed by elected officials
    b. individual citizens create, exchange, and control goods and resources
    c. charity, philanthropy, and volunteering decrease
    d. demand and supply are decided through majority vote
    e. government implements policies that favor businesses over consumers

26. Business profit is:

    a. cost minus revenue
    b. assets minus liabilities
    c. revenue minus expenses
    d. selling price of a stock minus its purchase price
    e. earnings minus assets

27. Free markets typically secure more economic prosperity than government's centralized planning because:

    a. the price system utilizes more local knowledge of

means and ends

b. markets rely upon coercion, whereas government relies upon voluntary compliance with the law

c. more tax revenue can be generated from free enterprise

d. property rights and contracts are best enforced by the market system

e. government planners are too cautious in spending taxpayers' money

28. A progressive tax:

a. encourages more investment from those with higher incomes

b. is illustrated by a 6% sales tax

c. requires those with higher incomes to pay a higher ratio of taxes to income

d. requires every income class to pay the same ratio of taxes to income

e. earmarks revenues for poverty reduction

29. A flood-control levee (or National Defense) is considered a public good because:

a. citizens value it as much as bread and medicine

b. a resident can benefit from it without directly paying for it

c. government construction contracts increase employment

d. insurance companies cannot afford to replace all houses after a flood

e. government pays for its construction, not citizens

30. Which of the following fiscal policy combinations has the federal government most often followed to stimulate economic activity when the economy is in a severe recession?

a. increasing both taxes and spending

b. increasing taxes and decreasing spending

c. decreasing taxes and increasing spending

d. decreasing both taxes and spending

31. International trade and specialization most often lead to which of the following?

a. an increase in a nation's productivity

b. a decrease in a nation's economic growth in the long term

c. an increase in a nation's import tariffs

d. a decrease in a nation's standard of living

32. Which of the following is a policy tool of the Federal Reserve?

a. raising or lowering income taxes

b. increasing or decreasing unemployment benefits

c. buying or selling government securities

d. increasing or decreasing government spending

33. If taxes equal government spending, then:

a. government debt is zero

b. printing money no longer causes inflation

c. government is not helping anybody

d. tax per person equals government spending per person on average

e. tax loopholes and special-interest spending are absent

Resource: http://www.isi.org/quiz

Answers To Full Civic Literacy Exam

1. Which of the following are the unalienable rights referred to in the Declaration of Independence?

(e) life, liberty, and the pursuit of happiness

2. In 1933 Franklin Delano Roosevelt proposed a series of government programs that became known as:

(c) the New Deal

3. What are the three branches of government?

(a) executive, legislative, judicial

4. What was the main issue in the debates between Abraham Lincoln and Stephen A. Douglas in 1858?

(b) would slavery be allowed to expand to new territories?

5. The United States Electoral College:

(d) is a constitutionally mandated assembly that elects the President

6. The Bill of Rights explicitly prohibits:

(d) establishing an official religion for the United States

7. What was the source of the following phrase: "Government of the people, by the people, for the people"?

(d) Gettysburg Address

8. In 1935 and 1936 the Supreme Court declared that important parts of the New Deal were unconstitutional. President Roosevelt responded by threatening to:

(c) appoint additional Supreme Court justices who shared his views

9. Under our Constitution, some powers belong exclusively to the federal government. What is one power of the federal government?

(a) make treaties

10. Name one right or freedom guaranteed by the first amendment.

(c) religion

11. What impact did the Anti-Federalists have on the United States Constitution?

(a) their arguments helped lead to the adoption of the Bill of Rights

12. Which of the following statements is true about abortion?

(b) the Supreme Court struck down most legal restrictions on it in Roe v. Wade

13. Plato, Aristotle, and Aquinas would concur that:

(e) certain permanent moral and political truths are accessible to human reason

14. The Puritans:

(b) stressed the sinfulness of all humanity

15. The phrase that in America there should be a "wall of separation" between church and state appears in:

(e) Thomas Jefferson's letters

16. In his "I Have a Dream" speech, Dr. Martin Luther King, Jr.:

(d) expressed his hopes for racial justice and brotherhood

17. Sputnik was the name given to the first:

(d) manmade satellite

18. Susan B. Anthony was a leader of the movement to:

(a) guarantee women the right to vote in national elections

19. The Scopes "Monkey Trial" was about:

(b) teaching evolution in the schools

20. Who is the commander-in-chief of the U.S. military?

(c) President

21. Name two countries that were our enemies during World War II.

(b) Germany and Japan

22. What part of the government has the power to declare war?

(a) Congress

23. In October 1962 the United States and the Soviet Union came close to war over the issue of Soviet:

(b) missiles in Cuba

24. In the area of United States foreign policy, Congress shares power with the:

(a) President

25. Free enterprise or capitalism exists insofar as:

(b) individual citizens create, exchange, and control goods and
resources

26. Business profit is:

(c) revenue minus expenses

27. Free markets typically secure more economic prosperity than government's centralized planning because:

(a) the price system utilizes more local knowledge of means and ends

28. A progressive tax:

(c) requires those with higher incomes to pay a higher ratio of taxes to income

29. A flood-control levee (or National Defense) is considered a public good because:

(b) a resident can benefit from it without directly paying for it

30. Which of the following fiscal policy combinations has the federal government most often followed to stimulate economic activity when the economy is in a severe recession?

(c) decreasing taxes and increasing spending

31. International trade and specialization most often lead to which of the following?

(a) an increase in a nation's productivity

32. Which of the following is a policy tool of the Federal Reserve?

(c) buying or selling government securities

33. If taxes equal government spending, then:

(d) tax per person equals government spending per person on average

Civics Questions for the Naturalization Test

The 100 civics (history and government) questions and answers for the Naturalization Test are listed below. The civics test is an oral test and the U.S.CIS Officer will ask the applicant up to 10 of the 100 civics questions. An applicant must answer 6 out of 10 questions correctly to pass the civics portion of the Naturalization Test.

On the Naturalization Test, some answers may change because of elections or appointments. The U.S. CIS Officer will not accept an incorrect answer.

Although U.S.CIS is aware that there may be additional correct answers to the 100 civics questions, applicants are encouraged to respond to the civics questions using the answers provided.

If you are 65 years old or older and have been a legal permanent resident of the United States for 20 or more years, you may study just the questions that have been marked with an asterisk.

American Government

PRINCIPLES OF AMERICAN DEMOCRACY

1. What is the supreme law of the land?

the Constitution

2. What does the Constitution do?

sets up the government
defines the government
protects basic rights of Americans

3. The idea of self-government is in the first three words of the Constitution. What are these words?

We the People

4. What is an amendment?

a change (to the Constitution)

an addition (to the Constitution)

5. What do we call the first ten amendments to the Constitution?

the Bill of Rights

6. What is one right or freedom from the First Amendment?

speech
religion
assembly
press
petition the government

7. How many amendments does the Constitution have?

twenty-seven (27)

8. What did the Declaration of Independence do?

announced our independence (from Great Britain)
declared our independence (from Great Britain)
said that the United States is free (from Great Britain)

9. What are two rights in the Declaration of Independence?

life
liberty
pursuit of happiness

10. What is freedom of religion?

you can practice any religion, or not practice a religion.

11. What is the economic system in the United States?*

economy
market economy

12. What is the "rule of law?"

everyone must follow the law
leaders must obey the law
government must obey the law
no one is above the law

SYSTEM OF GOVERNMENT

13. Name one branch or part of the government.*

Congress
legislative
President
executive
the courts
judicial

14. What stops one branch of government from becoming too powerful?

checks and balances
separation of powers

15. Who is in charge of the executive branch?

the President

16. Who makes federal laws?

Congress
Senate and House (of Representatives)
(U.S. or national) legislature

17. What are the two parts of the U.S. Congress?*

the Senate and House (of Representatives)

18. How many U.S. Senators are there?

one hundred (100)

19. We elect a U.S. Senator for how many years?

six (6)

20. Who is one of your state's U.S. Senators now?*

answers will vary

21. The House of Representatives has how many voting members?

four hundred thirty-five (435)

22. We elect a U.S. Representative for how many years?

two (2)

23. Name your U.S. Representative.

answers will vary

24. Who does a U.S. senator represent?

all people of the state

25. Why do some states have more representatives than other states?

(because of) the state's population
(because) they have more people
(because) some states have more people

26. We elect a President for how many years?

four (4)

27. In what month do we vote for President?*

November

28. What is the name of the President of the United States now?*

Barack Obama
Obama

29. What is the name of the Vice President of the United States *now?*

Joseph R. Biden, Jr.
Joe Biden
Biden

30. If the President can no longer serve, who becomes President?

the Vice President

31. If both the President and the Vice President can no longer serve, who becomes President?

the Speaker of the House

32. Who is the Commander in Chief of the military?

the President

33. Who signs bills to become laws?

the President

34. Who vetoes bills?

the President

35. What does the President's cabinet do?

advises the President

36. What are two cabinet-level positions?

Secretary of Agriculture
Secretary of Commerce
Secretary of Defense
Secretary of Education
Secretary of Energy
Secretary of Health and Human Services
Secretary of Homeland Security
Secretary of Housing and Urban Development
Secretary of the Interior
Secretary of Labor
Secretary of State
Secretary of Transportation
Secretary of the Treasury
Secretary of Veterans Affairs
Attorney General
Vice President

37. What does the judicial branch do?

reviews laws
explains laws
resolves disputes (disagreements)
decides if a law goes against the Constitution

38. What is the highest court in the United States?

the Supreme Court

39. How many justices are on the Supreme Court?

nine (9)

40. Who is the Chief Justice of the United States now?

John Roberts (John G. Roberts, Jr.)

41. Under our Constitution, some powers belong to the Federal government. What is one power of the Federal Government?

to print money
to declare war
to create an army
to make treaties

42. Under our Constitution, some powers belong to the states. What is one power of the states?

provide schooling and education
provide protection (police)
provide safety (fire departments)
give a driver's license
approve zoning and land use

43. Who is the governor of your state now?

answers will vary.

44. What is the capital of your state?*

answers will vary.

45. What are the two major political parties in the United States?*

Democratic and Republican

46. What is the political party of the President now?

Democratic (Party)

47. What is the name of the Speaker of the House of Representatives now?

John Boehner

RIGHTS AND RESPONSIBILITIES

48. There are four amendments to the Constitution about who can vote. Describe one of them.

citizens eighteen (18) and older (can vote)
you don't have to pay (a poll tax) to vote
any citizen can vote. (women and men can vote)
a male citizen of any race (can vote)

49. What is one responsibility that is only for United States citizens?*

serve on a jury
vote in a federal election

50. Name one right only for United States citizens.

vote in a federal election
run for federal office

51. What are two rights of everyone living in the United States?

freedom of expression
freedom of speech
freedom of assembly
freedom to petition the government
freedom of worship
the right to bear arms

52. What do we show loyalty to when we say the Pledge of Allegiance?

the United States
the flag

53. What is one promise you make when you become a United States citizen?

give up loyalty to other countries
defend the Constitution and laws of the United States
obey the laws of the United States
serve in the U.S. military (if needed)
serve (do important work for) the nation (if needed)
be loyal to the United States

54. How old do citizens have to be to vote for President?*

eighteen (18) and older

55. What are two ways that Americans can participate in their democracy?

vote
join a political party
help with a campaign
join a civic group
join a community group
give an elected official your opinion on an issue
call Senators and Representatives
publicly support or oppose an issue or policy
run for office
write to a newspaper

56. When is the last day you can send in federal income tax forms?*

April 15

57. When must all men register for the Selective Service?

at age eighteen (18)
between eighteen (18) and twenty-six (26)

AMERICAN HISTORY

COLONIAL PERIOD AND INDEPENDENCE

58. What is one reason colonists came to America?

freedom
political liberty
religious freedom
economic opportunity
practice their religion
escape persecution

59. Who lived in America before the Europeans arrived?

American Indians
Native Americans

60. What group of people was taken to America and sold as slaves?

Africans
people from Africa

61. Why did the colonists fight the British?

because of high taxes (taxation without representation)
because the British army stayed in their houses (boarding, quartering)
because they didn't have self-government

62. Who wrote the Declaration of Independence?

(Thomas) Jefferson

63. When was the Declaration of Independence adopted?

July 4, 1776

64. There were 13 original states. Name three.

New Hampshire
Massachusetts
Rhode Island
Connecticut
New York
New Jersey
Pennsylvania

65. What happened at the Constitutional Convention?

The Constitution was written
The Founding Fathers wrote the Constitution

66. When was the Constitution written?

1787

67. The Federalist Papers supported the passage of the U.S. Constitution. Name one of the writers.

(James) Madison
(Alexander) Hamilton
(John) Jay
Publius

68. What is one thing Benjamin Franklin is famous for?

U.S. diplomat
oldest member of the Constitutional Convention
first Postmaster General of the United States
writer of "Poor Richard's Almanac"
started the first free libraries

69. Who is the "Father of Our Country"?

(George) Washington

70. Who was the first President?*

(George) Washington

1800s

71. What territory did the United States buy from France in 1803?

> *the Louisiana Territory*
> *Louisiana*

72. Name one war fought by the United States in the 1800s.

> *War of 1812*
> *Mexican-American War*
> *Civil War*
> *Spanish-American War*

73. Name the U.S. war between the North and the South.

> *the Civil War*
> *the War Between the States*

74. Name one problem that led to the Civil War.

> *slavery*
> *economic reasons*
> *states' rights*

75. What was one important thing that Abraham Lincoln did?*

> *freed the slaves (Emancipation Proclamation)*
> *saved (or preserved) the Union*
> *led the United States during the Civil War*

76. What did the Emancipation Proclamation do?

> *freed the slaves*
> *freed slaves in the Confederacy*
> *freed slaves in the Confederate states*
> *freed slaves in most Southern states*

77. What did Susan B. Anthony do?

> *fought for women's rights*
> *fought for civil rights*

Recent American History and Other Important Historical Information

78. Name one war fought by the United States in the 1900s.*

World War I
World War II
Korean War
Vietnam War
(Persian) Gulf War

79. Who was President during World War I?

(Woodrow) Wilson

80. Who was President during the Great Depression and World War II?

(Franklin) Roosevelt

81. Who did the United States fight in World War II?

Japan, Germany, and Italy

82. Before he was President, Eisenhower was a general. What war was he in?

World War II

83. During the Cold War, what was the main concern of the United States?

Communism

84. What movement tried to end racial discrimination?

civil rights (movement)

85. What did Martin Luther King, Jr. do?*

fought for civil rights
worked for equality for all Americans

86. What major event happened on September 11, 2001 in the United States?

Terrorists attacked the United States.

87. Name one American Indian tribe in the United States.

[U.S.CIS officers will be supplied with a list of federally recognized American Indian tribes.]

Cherokee	*Choctaw*	*Iroquois*
Navajo	*Pueblo*	*Creek*
Sioux	*Apache*	*Blackfeet*
Seminole	*Mohegan*	*Crow*
Cheyenne	*Chippewa*	*Teton*
Arawak	*Huron*	*Hopi*
Shawnee	*Oneida*	*Inuit*
	Lakota	

INTERGRATED CIVICS

Geography

88. Name one of the two longest rivers in the United States.

Missouri (River)
Mississippi (River)

89. What ocean is on the West Coast of the United States?

Pacific (Ocean)

90. What ocean is on the East Coast of the United States?

Atlantic (Ocean)

91. Name one U.S. territory.

Puerto Rico
U.S. Virgin Islands
American Samoa
Northern Mariana Islands
Guam

92. Name one state that borders Canada.

Maine
New Hampshire
Minnesota
North Dakota
Montana
Idaho
Washington
Alaska
Vermont
New York
Pennsylvania
Ohio
Michigan

93. Name one state that borders Mexico.

California
Arizona
New Mexico
Texas

94. What is the capital of the United States?*

Washington, D.C.

95. Where is the Statue of Liberty?*

New York (Harbor)
Liberty Island
[Also acceptable are New Jersey, near New York City, and on the Hudson (River)]

Symbols

96. Why does the flag have 13 stripes?

because there were 13 original colonies
because the stripes represent the original colonies

97. Why does the flag have 50 stars?*

because there is one star for each state
because each star represents a state
because there are 50 states

98. What is the name of the national anthem?

The Star-Spangled Banner

Holidays

99. When do we celebrate Independence Day?*

July 4

100. Name two national U.S. holidays.

New Year's Day
Martin Luther King, Jr. Day
Presidents' Day
Memorial Day
Independence Day
Labor Day

Columbus Day
Veterans Day
Thanksgiving
Christmas

Resource: www.uscis.gov

NATURALIZATION

Naturalization is the process where a foreign born person becomes a citizen of the United States.

Depending on where and when you choose to file your application, the period of time between sending in the completed application and the interview to become a U.S. citizen can vary from five months to more than two years.

The swearing-in ceremony for receiving the naturalization certificate will then take place from 1 to 180 days after the interview, although in a few U.S. Citizenship and Immigration Services (U.S. CIS, formerly known as the INS) district offices, it can take another one or two years.

The length of time for the entire process depends on the number of U.S. citizenship applications the U.S.CIS offices receive in each state. Additionally, making a mistake on the application can cost even more time. However, by using the U.S. CIS unique do-it-yourself service, applicants will be assisted throughout the entire process — helping to prevent costly mistakes to the application.

Before applying to be a citizen, a permanent resident visa ("green card") (is needed).

There are only four ways to receive a green card:

1. Sponsorship by an American citizen or a permanent resident
2. Sponsorship by an employer
3. Marrying an American citizen or permanent resident
4. Winning the Green Card Lottery

After receiving a green card, one must live in the United States for five years in a row, or three years if married to a U.S. citizen.

When the three or five year waiting period is over, application to be a citizen can be made if the applicant is over eighteen years of age and has lived in the state of current residence for at least three months.

Once the application has been filed, the U.S. CIS begins an investigation and holds a hearing to determine whether the applicant arrived in the United States legally.

At the hearing, fitness for American citizenship is based on showing: a strong sense of morality; belief in democracy; support for the principles of American government; literacy in the English language; and knowledge of American history and government.

After passing the hearing, an oath will take place before a federal judge.

Naturalized citizens make three promises:

1. Loyalty to the American government, rather than to their former country
2. Living according to the laws, rules, and Constitution of the United States
3. Defending the United States, and if required, to serve in the military

When leaving the federal courthouse, the new citizen will have a certificate of naturalization and nearly identical rights to an American-born citizen.

AMERICAN HISTORY TIMELINE

The history of the American continent and its natives began long before it was colonized by the Europeans during the 1400s - 1600s. Native Americans are believed to have lived on this continent for over 10,000 years prior to the European voyagers' entry. 1607 is when the true history of the United States began with the establishment and consolidation of the thirteen British colonies along the eastern coast of the Continent.

The United States was born when these thirteen colonies revolted against the British throne, winning their freedom during the American Revolutionary War (1775-1783). From these thirteen colonies came the Declaration of Independence and the U.S. Constitution, which continue to be the foundation for the government, growth and success of our beautiful country.

BEFORE 1492 The first humans are believed to have arrived in North America over 10,000 years ago. They crossed a land bridge that existed between Asia and North America in the area that is now the Bering Straits. The Native Americans developed individual groups or nations. It is estimated that when the first Europeans arrived in 1492 there were 15 to 20 million Native Americans living in the land. They spoke over 1,000 languages.

1492 Christopher Columbus made the first of four voyages to the New World, funded by the king of Spain. Looking for a western sea route to Asia, his ship, Santa Maria, landed in the Bahamas on October 12. Columbus thought he had found a Japanese island and never knew he had discovered a new continent. Thinking he had found a new route to Asia and had reached the Indies, Columbus called the natives of the new land Indians. Those Indians were actually Tainos, native people of the Caribbean islands.

1499 Not everyone in Europe believed that Columbus had landed in Asia, including Italian navigator, Amerigo Vespucci, who, while sailing for Spain, landed in the same place as Columbus. He continued his trip and discovered the coast of South America. Two years later the king of Portugal sent Vespucci on another voyage in which he traveled from present-day Venezuela to Argentina.

1507 The name "America," for Amerigo Vespucci, was first used referring to the New World.

1513 Searching for the Fountain of Youth on Bimini Island, Spanish explorer Juan Ponce de Leon landed instead in Florida. He was the first Spaniard to set foot in what became the United States. Calusa Indians attacked him when he tried to start a settlement in Florida.

1565 The Spanish founded the first permanent European colony in North America in St. Augustine, Florida.

1606 A Virginia charter granted by England's King James I established the London Company and the Plymouth Company, made up of men from those two English cities. The companies were authorized to establish settlements at least 100 miles apart in the New World.

1607 Jamestown, Virginia was founded on May 14 by Captain Christopher Newport of the London Company. By the end of that year, starvation and disease reduced the original 105 settlers to 32. Captain John Smith was captured by Chief Powhatan and saved by the chief's daughter, Pocahontas.

1608 In January, 110 colonists arrived in Jamestown. In December of that year, lumber and iron, the first items of export from Jamestown, were sent to England.

1619 The first session of the first legislative assembly in America was convened in the Virginia House of Burgesses in Jamestown. Twenty-two burgesses, or agents of the people, represented 11 plantations.

Twenty Africans were brought to Jamestown on a Dutch ship and offered for sale as indentured servants, marking the beginning of slavery in Colonial America.

1620 The ship Mayflower arrived at Cape Cod, Massachusetts on November 9 with 101 colonists. Two days later the Mayflower Compact was signed by 41 men, establishing a form of local government in which colonists agreed to abide by majority rule and to cooperate for the general good of the colony. The compact set precedent for other colonies as they formed governments.

1690 The Massachusetts Bay colony issued the first paper money in the colonies. Until that time, money consisted of gold and silver coins from England, Spain and other countries. For many years, the Spanish dollar coin served as the "unofficial" national currency of the American colonies. As trading started between the settlements and coins became scarce, many colonies printed their own colonial notes

1692 The Salem Witch Trials took place in Salem Village, Massachusetts. Hysteria over suspected witchcraft practices led to 19 victims of the witch-hunt being hanged. One was crushed to death under the weight of stones, and at least four died in prison awaiting trial.

1697 The Massachusetts General Court expressed official regret for the actions of its judges during the witch hysteria of 1692. Jurors signed a statement of regret, and compensation was offered to the families of the wrongly accused.

1700 In June, Massachusetts, followed by New York, passed a law ordering all Roman Catholic priests to leave the colony within three months upon penalty of life imprisonment or execution. France and England struggled for dominance of the North American continent.

1701 The French established a settlement at Detroit in July.

1718 New Orleans was established by the French.

1720 The population of the American colonies reached 475,000. Boston was the largest city with a population of 12,000, followed by Philadelphia, with a population of 10,000 and New York with 7,000.

1725 The population of African slaves in the colonies reached 75,000.

1729 Benjamin Franklin began publishing the Pennsylvania Gazette, which eventually became the most popular colonial newspaper.

1730 Jewish colonists in New York City built the first American synagogue.

1731 The first American public library was founded in Philadelphia by Benjamin Franklin.

1747 The New York Bar Association was founded.

1751 The English Parliament passed the Currency Act, banning the issuance of paper money by the colonists and effectively assuming control of the currency system in the colonies.

1752 The first general hospital was founded in Philadelphia.

1754-63 The war between Great Britain and France, known as the French and Indian War, erupted as the result of a dispute over the area where present-day Pittsburgh exists and was fought along a corridor from Virginia to Nova Scotia. The outcome was that France ceded French Louisiana west of the Mississippi River to Spain as compensation for Spain's loss of Florida to Britain, greatly reducing France's colonial presence in America. Great Britain became the dominant colonial power in the eastern half of North America.

1760 The population of colonists in America reached 1,500,000. In March much of Boston was destroyed by fire.

1763 The Proclamation of 1763, signed by King George III of England, forbade English settlement west of the Appalachian Mountains and required those already settled in those regions to return, in an effort to ease tensions with Native Americans.

1765 The Stamp Act was passed by English Parliament, which imposed the first direct tax on the American colonies, to offset the rising costs of the British military in America. Under this act, all printed materials were taxed including newspapers, bills, legal documents, pamphlets, licenses, almanacs, dice and playing cards. The colonists opposed the tax, and on November 1, the day the tax was to go into effect, most businesses closed in protest.

1766 King George repealed the Stamp Act.

1770 The population of the American colonies reached 2,210,000.

1773 Bostonians, disguised as Mohawk Indians, boarded the British ships docked in Boston Harbor and dumped 340 chests of tea into the water in protest of the tax levied on tea by the English government. This became known as the Boston Tea Party.

1774 The first Continental Congress met in Philadelphia, with 56 delegates representing every state except Georgia. Delegates included Patrick Henry, George Washington and Samuel Adams.

Patriots began going from protesting government to overthrowing it throughout the colonies. They dismissed British authority and assumed political control of town meetings and county conventions.

1775 Midnight riders warned Massachusetts colonists of the arrival of the British.

The first battles of the American Revolution took place at Lexington and Concord, Massachusetts on April 18 and 19.

George Washington was officially appointed commander in chief of the Continental Army.

The Continental Congress authorized the limited printing of paper notes, known as "continentals," to finance the Revolutionary War.

1775-1783 The American Revolutionary War, also known as the American War of Independence, lasted 8 years. The war was the culmination of the political American Revolution in which the colonists overthrew British rule.

1776 The Second Continental Congress adopted the Declaration of Independence on July 4.

In January Thomas Paine published "Common Sense," a book using reason to convince the divided colonies to seek independence from the British monarchy.

George Washington, encamped with the Continental Army along the Pennsylvania shore of the Delaware River on December 25, decided to cross the ice-swollen Delaware during the night and attack the Hessian garrison defending Trenton at daybreak. The surprise attack was victorious and many believe was the turning point in the Revolutionary War for the colonials. Despite the victory, the weather was horrendous and prevented him from continuing on to Princeton. He retraced his steps back across the Delaware taking his Hessian prisoners with him. But news of the victory spread rapidly, rekindling the spirit of the colonials. On December 30 Washington again crossed the Delaware, attacked and won another victory at Trenton on January 2, and then pushed on to Princeton defeating the British there on January 3.

1779 Thomas Jefferson was elected governor of Virginia. He served two successive terms.

1781 British General Cornwallis surrendered 7,247 troops at Yorktown. General Washington, with help from Marie-Joseph Paul Roch Ives Gilbert du Motier, Marquis de Lafayette and other French officers, had effectively won independence for the colonies.

1782 Virginia legislators passed a law permitting the freeing of slaves.

1783 The American Revolutionary War officially ended on September 3, when the United States and Great Britain signed the definitive peace treaty in Paris.

1787 The Constitutional Convention, made up of delegates from 12 of the original 13 colonies, met in Philadelphia to draft the U.S. Constitution. This document defined the workings of the new American government, giving the federal government limited power and placing importance on our basic individual rights.

1789 George Washington became the first President of the United States and appointed Alexander Hamilton the first Secretary of the Treasury. Hamilton consolidated America's debts and paid them fairly, established a modern finaancial system and argued for an economy that included manufacturing as well as farming.

1790 The U.S. Supreme Court met for the first time at the Merchants Exchange Building in New York City.

1791 The Bill of Rights was created to safeguard various fundamental rights that the early Americans wanted to be sure the government could not intrude upon.

Congress established the First Bank of the United States, giving it power to operate as the U.S. Treasury's fiscal agent and authorizing it to issue paper bank notes. The idea of a central bank was conceived by Alexander Hamilton.

1792 The nation's first financial credit crisis occurred due to the speculation of William Duer and Alexander Macomb against stock held by the Bank of New York, causing a run on banks. Alexander Hamilton bailed out the troubled banks with hundreds of thousands of dollars in securities.

1800 Spain restored Louisiana to France by the Treaty of San Ildefonso in October.

1803 The Louisiana Purchase — the western territory was acquired from France. President Jefferson sent James Monroe to assist Robert R. Livingston in purchasing the territory at the mouth of the Mississippi, including the island of New Orleans, from Napoleon. Instead, they found Napoleon willing to dispose of the entire province of Louisiana. The territory encompassed all or part of 15 current U.S. states and 2 Canadian provinces. The land purchased contained all of present-day Arkansas, Missouri, Iowa, Oklahoma, Kansas, Nebraska, parts of Minnesota that were west of the Mississippi River, most of North Dakota, nearly all of South Dakota, northeastern New Mexico, northern Texas, the portions of Montana, Wyoming, and Colorado east of the Continental Divide, and Louisiana west of the Mississippi

River, including the city of New Orleans. (Parts of this area were still claimed by Spain at the time of the Purchase). In addition, the Purchase contained small portions of land that would eventually become part of the Canadian provinces of Alberta and Saskatchewan. The purchase doubled the size of the United States.

Marbury v. Madison is a landmark 1803 case that helped define the "checks and balances" of the American form of government. William Marbury was appointed Justice of the Peace in the District of Columbia by President John Adams, but when his commission was not delivered, Marbury petitioned the Supreme Court to force Secretary of State James Madison to deliver the documents. The Supreme Court under Chief Justice John Marshall denied Marbury's petition, holding that the basis of his claim, the Judiciary Act of 1789, was unconstitutional. It was the first time in Western history that a court invalidated a law by declaring it "unconstitutional," a process now called "judicial review." This decision formed the basis for the implementation of judicial review in the United States under Article III of the U.S. Constitution.

1814 Francis Scott Key wrote the *Star Spangled Banner* as he watched the British attack Fort McHenry.

1816 The Second Bank of the United States was established by Congress.

1817-18 Gen. Andrew Jackson led a U.S. Army campaign against the Seminole Indians in East Florida to stop Seminole attacks on Georgia settlements in the first Seminole War. The United States virtually controlled East Florida following the war.

1819-1821 Through the terms of the Adams-Onis Treaty, Spain relinquished Florida to the United States in exchange for $5 million and relinquishment of any claims on Texas that they might have from the Louisiana Purchase.

1820 The Missouri Compromise, was formulated. It was an agreement between pro- and anti-slavery members of Congress that regulated slavery in the western territories. It prohibited slavery in the unorganized territory of the Great Plains and allowed it Missouri and the Arkansas Territory.

1823 The Monroe Doctrine was a policy established by President James Monroe in his State of the Union Address to Congress on Dec. 2, during which he said that further efforts by European countries to colonize land or interfere with states in the Americas would be viewed as acts of aggression and consequently be met with retaliation. While asserting that the Americas were not to be further colonized by European countries, he stated that neither would the United States interfere with existing European colonies nor meddle in the internal affairs of European countries. Although a defining moment in establishing the foreign policy of the United States, Monroe's statement did not become known as the Monroe Doctrine until the 1850s.

1828 The Tariff of 1828, passed by Congress on May 19, was designed to protect industry in the northern United States. However, southern states were negatively impacted directly by having to pay higher prices on goods the region did not produce and indirectly by losing cotton revenues that the British could no longer afford because of the reduction in British goods to the United States as a result of the high tariffs imposed on them.

1832 President Andrew Jackson vetoed the re-charter of the Second Bank. The Free Banking Era followed the demise of the First and Second Banks of the United States, marking a quarter century in which American banking was a hodgepodge of state-chartered banks without federal regulation. By 1860, an estimated 8,000 different state banks were circulating worthless currency called "wildcat" or "broken" bank notes, so called because many of these banks were located in remote regions and frequently failed.

1836 On March 2 Texas seceded from Mexico. The newly independent Republic of Texas lasted until 1845 when the territory formally became a U.S. state.

1837 Speculative fever caused a financial crisis when a national panic created bank failures, a 5-year depression, and record-high unemployment.

1847 Samuel Morse formed the first telegraph company in the United States.

1848 Gold was discovered at John Sutter's Mill, and the California Gold Rush began.

Treaty of peace with Mexico transfered New Mexico and California to the U.S.

1855 The first American oil company, the Pennsylvania Rock Oil Company, was formed.

1857 Following several prosperous years, many banks, merchants, and farmers had taken risks with their investments, but when market prices began to fall, another financial panic occurred. Although the crisis was short-lived, it caused the failure of the Ohio Life Insurance and Trust Company, followed by business failures and a decline in the railroad industry, which resulted in hundreds of layoffs.

The Dred Scott Decision (Dred Scott v. Sanford) was the Supreme Court ruling that found any person of African ancestry could not claim citizenship in the United States. Scott unsuccessfully sued for his freedom along with his wife and two daughters, claiming that, although he and his wife were slaves, they had lived with their master in states and territories where slavery was illegal. The Supreme Court's ruling found that since Scott was not a U.S. citizen he could not file suit in federal court. Instead of settling Congressional authority and issues related to slavery, the decision created outrage and increased tensions over the slavery debate, eventually leading to the Emancipation Proclamation, the Thirteenth, Fourteenth and Fifteenth Amendments to the U.S. Constitution.

1858 The Lincoln-Douglas Debates were a series of seven debates between Abraham Lincoln, Republican candidate for the Illinois Senate, and the incumbent Senator Stephen Douglas, the Democratic Party candidate. Because U.S. senators were elected by state legislatures at the time, the candidates were competing for control of the Illinois legislature by their respective party. The main issue argued in all seven debates was slavery. Lincoln lost the Senate election but gained enough popularity from the press coverage of the debates to be nominated for President in 1860.

1860 The Pony Express began ten-day service from Missouri to Sacramento.

1861 The Civil War began, born out of conflict between the North and South (the Confederacy) over the expansion of slavery into the western states.

Congress approved the first federal income tax, 3 % levy on incomes over $800.

1862 Slavery was abolished in the District of Columbia.

1863 The Emancipation Proclamation went into effect January 1, freeing persons held as slaves within the rebellious states.

Passage of the National Bank Act established a national banking system and a uniform national currency to be issued by new "national" banks. The banks were required to purchase U.S. government securities as backing for their national bank notes.

The Battle of Gettysburg, the bloodiest battle of the Civil War took place at Gettysburg, Pennsylvania from July 1-3, 1863 and is generally considered to be the turning point of the American Civil War.

The Gettysburg Address was a historic speech made by President Abraham Lincoln on the battle site at Gettysburg, Pennsylvania 4 months (Nov. 19) after the Battle of Gettysburg.

1865 Congress approved the Thirteenth Amendment to the Constitution, which prohibited slavery in the United States. The Civil War ended. Abraham Lincoln was assassinated.

1867 Russia sold Alaska to the United States for $7.2 million on March 30.

1870 The Industrial Revolution began in America.

1873 The Fourth Coinage Act embraced the gold standard and demonetized silver, causing a fall in demand of silver internationally, which in turn started a severe international economic depression, known as The Long Depression, in both Europe and the United States that lasted until 1879. In America, a number of railroads, including the St. Paul & Pacific Railroad, went bankrupt.

1878 Authorized by the Bland–Allison Act, the Morgan Silver Dollar was the first standard silver dollar minted since production of that denomination ceased due to the passage of the Fourth Coinage Act in 1873.

1882 John D. Rockefeller organized the Standard Oil Trust.

1883 The Brooklyn Bridge between New York and Brooklyn was completed.

1884 The Recession of 1882-85 culminated in a national panic when European gold reserves were depleted. Approved by the U.S. Treasury, national banks in New York City halted investments in the rest of the United States and called in outstanding loans. The investment firm of Grant & Ward, Marine Bank of New York, and Penn Bank of Pittsburgh, along with more than 10,000 small firms failed despite a bailout of at-risk banks by New York Clearing House
.

1886 The Statue of Liberty, a gift from France, was dedicated on October 28, and placed in New York Harbor. It stands as a symbol of freedom throughout the world.

The American Federation of Labor was established in Columbus, Ohio. It comprises twenty-five labor groups representing 150,000 members.

1893 A severe economic depression began in the United States due to overbuilding, shaky financing in the railroad industry and a run on gold supplies. the run was caused by the Silver Purchase Act, which required the government to increase the amount of silver it was required to purchase each month.

1898 The U.S. Battleship Maine was destroyed on February 15 in Havana, Cuba, killing 260 on board. The cause was never determined but it was one of the precipitating events of the Spanish-American War.

1901 The first stock market crash on the New York Stock Exchange occurred.

1905 Telephone service was established between New York and Boston, the first "long distance."

Boston completed the first U.S. subway.

1906 An earthquake hit San Francisco, destroying the business districts and much of the city and leaving 250,000 people homeless, 25,000 buildings destroyed, and 500 dead.

1907 A severe bank panic created a financial crisis when the New York Stock Exchange fell close to 50% from its peak the previous year. Known as the 1907 Bankers' Panic, it fueled the reform movement to create a central bank, which would eventually lead to the creation of the Federal Reserve System.

1908 The first production Model T was sold by Henry Ford.

1913 President Woodrow Wilson signed the Federal Reserve Act on December 23. The Act established the Federal Reserve System to oversee the nation's money supply and empowered it to issue Federal Reserve notes.

The parcel post system is placed in operation.

Ford introduced the assembly line.

1914 The U.S. Stock Exchange was closed shortly after the beginning of World War I on July 31, partially re-opened on November 28 in order to help the war effort by trading bonds, and completely reopened for stock trading in mid-December.

The Panama Canal opened.

1915 The first telephone conversation was held from New York to San Francisco on January 25 between Alexander Graham Bell and Thomas A. Watson.

1916 The United States bought the Virgin Islands from Denmark on August 4.

1917 World War I - began when the United States formally declared war on Germany on April 6. The first U.S. troops arrived in Europe on June 26.

1918 World War I ended on November 11.

1919 Prohibition; ratification of the Eighteenth Amendment to the U.S. Constitution (Jan. 16) prohibited the manufacture, sale, transportation, and/or importation of intoxicating liquors in the United States. The Volstead Act was passed on Oct. 18th by Congress to enforce the law. However, most large cities lacked interest in enforcing the law and, while alcohol consumption did decline, there was a dramatic rise in organized crime in large cities to capitalize on a commodity created by the legislation that was in the high demand.

1920 The 19th Amendment to the Constitution was placed into law on August 26 giving women the right to vote.

1924 Congress approved a law on June 15 making all Indians United States citizens. That same year the first woman governor, Nellie Taylor Ross, was elected in Wyoming on November 6.

1925 Henry Ford started commercial airplane service between Detroit and Chicago.

1926 A highly destructive Florida hurricane caused the collapse of the land boom.

1927 Captain Charles A. Lindbergh landed his plane, the Spirit of St. Louis, in Paris on May 21, completing the first non-stop solo flight across the Atlantic Ocean. The flight, which originated in New York, took 33.5 hours and encompassed 3,610 miles.

1928 Amelia Earhart became the first woman to fly across the Atlantic on June 17.

1929 The stock market crashed following a decade-long speculation of being able to gain wealth through investing. When stock prices began to fall it caused mass panic and massive selling of stocks and bonds. This resulted in the worst economic disaster in American history and marked the beginning of the Great Depression.

1932 Unable to raise fresh funds from the Federal Reserve System, banks failed by the hundreds.

1930 The Smoot-Hawley Tariff, aka the Tariff Act of 1930, raised tariffs on over 20,000 imported goods to overall levels that were the second highest in U.S. history (exceeded only by the Tariff of 1828). It was an attempt by the federal government to be a major intervention in the economy following the stock market crash of 1929 but had an adverse effect. Unemployment rates shot beyond levels it reached in the wake of the stock market crash, hitting an all-time high of 11.6% in November.

1933 The Glass-Steagall Act, aka the Banking Act of 1933, was passed to stabilize and rebuild the nation's failed economy during the Great Depression. It expanded the regulatory powers of the Federal Reserve, prohibited banks from trading in corporate securities, and created the Federal Deposit Insurance Corporation (FDIC), a government-run mechanism that insured bank depositors against bank failure.

The 21st Amendment repealed Prohibition in the United States with its passage on December 5th by giving states the right to establish their own laws concerning the control of alcohol.

1935 Congress passed the Banking Act of 1935 which altered the Federal Reserve's structure by creating the Federal Open Market Committee to oversee the conduct of monetary policy, adding stability to the banking system.

1936 Hoover Dam is completed.

1937 Amelia Earhart attempted to circumnavigate the globe, but disappeared somewhere in the Pacific on July 2 during the final leg of her solo flight.

1939 The first commercial television broadcast was aired.

1941 World War II began when Japan attacked Pearl Harbor in Hawaii on December 7. Nineteen ships were sunk or damaged, and

2,300 people died. Within three days, the United States was at war with Japan, Italy and Germany.

1945 Germany surrendered to the Allied Forces on May 8 and Japan surrendered on August 15.

The Instrument of Surrender was signed aboard the USS Missouri in Tokyo Bay on September 2.

1947 On Mar. 12, President Harry S. Truman announced what became known as the Truman Doctrine. The doctrine's purpose was to specifically support Greece and Turkey with economic and military aid to prevent them from falling into control of the Soviet Union. However, Truman also intended to establish a policy of the United States of offering economic and military aid to free people resisting attempts to overthrow their governments by armed minorities or outside pressures.

Taft-Hartley Act, aka the Labor-Management Relations Act, was enacted June 23. It's purpose was to monitor the activities and power of labor unions.

1948-52 The Marshall Plan was implemented officially called the European Recovery Program (ERP), it was a large-scale American program to aid Europe with monetary support to help rebuild European economies after the end of World War II. The goal of the United States was to rebuild a war-devastated region, remove trade barriers, modernize industry, and make Europe prosperous once again while preventing the spread of Soviet communism. Named after Secretary of State George Marshall, the plan was largely the creation of State Department officials that gained bi-partisan support from a Republican controlled Congress and Democratic White House.

1950-53 The years of the Korean War, The Korean peninsula was ruled by Japan from 1910 until the end of World War II. Following Japan's surrender in 1945, the Korean peninsula was divided along the 38th Parallel with U.S. troops occupying the southern part and Soviet troops occupying the northern part. This physical division of Korea eventually led to war between South Korea, supported by the United Nations, and North Korea, supported by the People's Republic of China, with military armament from the Soviet Union. Open warfare began when North Korean forces invaded South Korea on June 25, 1950 and ended with an armistice signed on July 27, 1953.

1954 On May 17, the Supreme Court unanimously ruled that racial segregation in public schools was unconstitutional and that it violated the 14th Amendment clause guaranteeing equal protection of the laws.

1955-75 The military conflict called the Vietnam War was fought between the governments of North Vietnam, supported by the Soviet Union and other communist nations, and South Vietnam, supported by the United States and other democratic nations, in Vietnam, Laos, and Cambodia from Nov. 1, 1955 until the fall of Saigon on April 30, 1975.

1956 The first transatlantic telephone cable was put into operation on September 25.

1957 The first Japanese car, a Toyota, was sold in the U.S.

1958 Explorer I, the first United States earth satellite, was launched into orbit by the army on January 31 at Cape Canaveral, Florida.

Eisenhower signed the act creating NASA.

Bank of America launched the first credit card.

1959 Alaska was admitted as the 49th state on January 3. Hawaii was admitted as the 50th state on August 21.

1962 President Kennedy informed the public of the Soviet

Union's offensive missile buildup in Cuba. He ordered air and naval quarantine of the island and demanded immediate dismantling of the weapons. Kennedy negotiated with Soviet Premier Nikita Khrushchev to end the Cuban Missile Crisis a week later.

The first WalMart opened.

1963 The Supreme Court ruled on June 17 that laws requiring the Lord's Prayer or bible verses in public schools were unconstitutional.

On August 28 Dr. Martin Luther King, Jr. led 200,000 Americans in a march on Washington, D.C. demanding equal rights.

President John Kennedy was shot and killed on November 22 in Dallas, Texas. Lyndon B. Johnson was sworn in as the 36th President of the United States.

1964 Congress passed the Civil Rights Bill on July 2. President Johnson signed the bill on the same day, banning any discrimination in voting, employment and any public accommodations.

The Medicare Bill was signed on July 30 establishing government health insurance for people over age 65.

1965 Dr. Martin Luther King, Jr. led a march from Selma to Montgomery, Alabama, demanding federal protection of the voting rights of black Americans.

American ground forces became directly involved in the Vietnam War between 1965 and 1973

1966 Edward Brooke of Massachusetts was elected the first black United States Senator in 85 years on November 8.

1967 Thurgood Marshall became the first African-American justice on the Surpreme Court.

1968 Dr. Martin Luther King, Jr. was assassinated on April 4 in Memphis, Tennessee. James Earl Ray, an escaped convict, pled guilty to the crime and was sentenced to 99 years in prison.

Senator Robert F. Kennedy of New York was shot on June 5 in Los Angeles. He died the next day. Sirhan Bishara Sirhan, a Jordanian, was convicted of the murder.

1969 Vietnam peace talks began on January 18.

American astronaut Neil Armstrong, commander of the Appolo 11 mission, became the first person to set foot on the moon.

1970 The first Earth Day celebration took place on April 22 in an effort to save the environment.

1973 Vietnam peace pacts were signed in Paris. The end of the military draft was announced on January 27.

Gerald R. Ford became the first vice-president to be appointed under the 26th Amendment after Spiro Agnew resigned, pleading no contest to charges of tax evasion.

Federal Express began operations.

1974 President Nixon resigned from office following charges of criminal conspiracy and obstruction of justice in the Watergate cover-up.

Gerald R. Ford became the 38th President and the only non-elected President of the United States. He issued an unconditional pardon to President Nixon for all federal crimes he may have committed.

1976 The United States celebrated 200 years of independence.

1980 The Depository Institutions Deregulation and Monetary Control Act (DIDMCA) was passed, abolishing state caps on interest rates that could be charged for primary mortgages, giving banks the incentive to approve mortgages for people with problematic credit histories.

1981 Sandra Day O'Connor was appointed as an associate justice of the United States Supreme Court, the first woman appointed to that body.

1983 Sally Ride became the first American woman to travel in space when the space shuttle Challenger was launched from Cape Canaveral, Florida.

1985 The federal government became debt-free for the first time.

1986 The space shuttle Challenger exploded moments after liftoff on January 28, killing six astronauts and New Hampshire teacher Christa McAuliffe.

1990-91 Operation Desert Storm, aka the Gulf War, aka the Persian Gulf War, commenced. This was a war waged by a U.N.-authorized coalition force from 34 nations led by the United States against Iraq in response to Iraq's invasion and occupation of Kuwait.

1991 The Strategic Arms Reduction Treaty was signed. With the fall of the Soviet Union it called for dramatic reductions in long-range nuclear weapons in the United States and the Soviet Union.

1992 The World Wide Web became available for use in the home.

Carol Moseley Braun became the first black woman elected to the United States Senate.

1993 President Bill Clinton hosted Israel's Prime Minister Yitzhak Rabin and Palestine Liberation Organization Chairman Yasir Arafat in Washington, D.C. during which Rabin and Arafat shook hands on the lawn of the White House.

The World Trade Center in New York was bombed.

1994 A violent earthquake shook the city of Los Angeles.

The Riegle-Neal Interstate Banking and Branching Efficiency Act (IBBEA) eliminated state barriers to interstate banking, allowing financial institutions to locate branches in other states and to purchase or merge with banks headquartered in other states.

1995 The first domestic terrorist attack occurred when a car bomb destroyed the federal building in Oklahoma City, Oklahoma.

1998 President Bill Clinton was impeached by the House of Representatives as a result of indescretions with a young female White House intern and found not guilty by the Senate of perjury and obstruction of justice.

1999 The Gramm-Leach-Bliley Act (GLBA), aka the Financial Services Modernization Act, repealed part of Glass-Steagall, allowing companies to merge, partner and operate freely within each other's industries. It also made it possible for the financial industry to group mortgage and other portfolios to sell them as investments.

2001 On September 11, Islamic terrorists hijacked and crashed four United States passenger airliners: two into the World Trade Center Twin Towers in New York City; one into the Pentagon in Washington, D.C.; and the one into the ground outside Pittsburgh, Pennsylvania. Estimates are that over 13,000 people were either killed or injured in the attacks on America.

On September 19, during a joint session of Congress, President George W. Bush announced plans for a war on terrorism around the world.

2002 In his State of the Union address on January 29 President Bush vowed to expand the fight on terrorism and labeled Iran, Iraq, and North Korea "an axis of evil."

Pennsylvania miners were rescued on July 28 after spending 77 hours in a dark, flooded mineshaft.

2003 The Iraq War began following President Bush's January 28 State of the Union address announcing that he was ready to attack Iraq even without a U.N. mandate. He claimed the Iraqis were hiding weapons of mass destruction, a claim that was later proved untrue.

Saddam Hussein was captured by American troops on December 13.

Space shuttle Columbia exploded on February 1, killing all 7 astronauts.

California governor Gray Davis was ousted in a recall vote, and actor Arnold Schwarzenegger was elected in his place.

2004 A rover landed on Mars on January 3. A second rover, Opportunity, landed on Mars January 25 and sent pictures to Earth. NASA later announced that the robot explorer Opportunity had detected signs that water had once covered the rocks of a small crater there.

President Bush, in his State of the Union address, defended action in Iraq and highlighted the urgency to continue fighting terrorism.

2005 Hurricane Katrina wrought catastrophic damage on the Gulf Coast; more than 1,000 people died and millions were left homeless. Americans are shaken not simply by the magnitude of the disaster but by how ill-prepared all levels of government were in its aftermath.

2006 Saddam Hussein was executed by hanging after the Iraqi High Tribunal found him guilty of crimes against humanity.

2008 The first African American, Barack Obama was elected President of the United States.

The worst financial crisis since the Great Depression caused the collapse of large financial institutions, an enormous downturn in the stock market, and a decline in the housing market resulting in massive evictions and foreclosures. The crisis was triggered by reduced interest rates, followed by easy credit, sub-prime lending, increased debt burden, incorrect pricing of risk, overall misconduct in the financial industry, conflicts of interest, and a liquidity shortfall in the United States banking system. These factors caused the crisis to rapidly spread throughout the world. The United States Senate's Levin–Coburn Report found that "High risk lending, regulatory failures, inflated credit ratings, and Wall Street firms engaging in massive conflicts of interest, contaminated the U.S. financial system with toxic mortgages and undermined public trust in U.S. markets."

2009 After weeks of deliberation President Barack Obama announced that he was ordering an additional 30,000 troops to Afghanistan in an attempt to prevent further Taliban insurgencies. He also announced that a year after the troops arrived, a transition would begin to hand off responsibility for the war to the Afghanistan army.

Sonia Sotomayor became the first Hispanic justice on the U.S. Supreme Court.

2010 On August 31, seven years after the war in Iraq began, President Obama announced the end of Operation Iraqi Freedom with the withdrawal of combat troops by the end of 2011.

On November 2, Republican candidates won the majority of elections, taking control of the U.S. House of Representatives, and taking over many governorships and other legislative bodies. This tide was the biggest turnaround in Congressional seats since 1948.

The Dodd-Frank Wall Street Reform and Consumer Protection Act of 2010 was created in response to a severe financial crisis that led to the Great Recession of 2007-09. Signed into law by President Barack Obama on July 21, the Dodd-Frank Act was the most extensive and comprehensive regulatory reform legislation since the early 1930s.

2011 On May 2, Osama bin Laden, mastermind of the 9/11 2001 attacks on the World Trade Center, the Pentagon, and other locations and leader of the terrorist group, Al Qaeda, was killed. It was the culmination of ten years of pursuit by United States and coalition forces and involved a raid by U.S. Navy Seals on his hideout location in Pakistan.

Sources:

"Founders: the People Who Brought You A Nation," Ray Raphael, MJF Books, New York, NY, 2009

U.S. Senate Committee on Banking, Housing, and Urban Affairs, www.senate.gov, 2009

"Levin-Coburn Report," United States Senate Homeland Security and governmental Affairs Committee, 13 April 2011

http://www.frbsf.org, Federal Reserve Bank of San Francisco, 2011

"Panic on Wall Street: A History of America's Financial Disasters," Robert Sobel, Beard Books, 1999

HOW GOVERNMENT WORKS

FEDERAL GOVERNMENT

The cornerstone of American government is the Constitution.
It is the highest law in the land and belongs to all
Americans. The Constitution states how government works,
creates the Presidency, Congress, and the Supreme Court.

The Constitution sets up three separate branches of
government with their own responsibilities.

The three branches of the U.S. government are the
Legislative, Executive, and Judicial.

Legislative Branch

Congress has two parts, the House of Representatives and the Senate.
The most important duty of Congress is to write, debate, and pass bills,
which are sent to the President for approval. Each Congress lasts for two
years. Congress meets once every year at the Capitol in Washington,
DC, usually from January 3 to July 31. Representation in the House
of Representatives is based on a state's population. Representation in
the Senate is equal for all states.

House of Representatives

There are 435 representatives in the House. Each representative serves a term of 2 years. When a term is over, the people may elect a new representative or keep the same one. There is no limit on the number of terms a representative can serve. States with larger populations have more representation than less populated states. Each state has at least one congressional district and therefore one representative in the House.

Requirements

A representative must be:

- at least 25 years old
- a U.S. citizen for the past 7 years
- a resident in the state they represent

The Senate

There is a total of 100 senators because each state sends 2 people to the Senate. Each senator serves a term of 6 years. When a term is over, the people may elect a new senator or keep the same one. There is no limit on the number of terms a senator can serve.

Requirements

A senator must be:

- at least 30 years old
- a U.S. citizen for the past 9 years
- live in the state they represent

Executive Branch

The Executive Branch includes the President, vice president, cabinet members, and heads of independent agencies. It is the duty of this branch to enforce laws of the United States.

The Presidency

The President of the United States is in charge of the Executive Branch. The President is leader of our country and commands the military. The President's job is to approve bills that Congress creates. If in agreement with the bill, the President signs it into law. If the President is not in agreement, the bill can be vetoed (refused to be signed). Congress can override a veto with a two-thirds vote.

The President serves as the American head of state and chief of the government. The President meets with leaders of other countries and can make treaties. He is technically the boss of every government worker and serves a term of four years. There is a two-term limit.

Requirements

The President must:

- be at least 35 years old
- be a natural-born U.S. citizen
- have lived in the U.S. for at least 14 years

Order of Succession

If the President of the United States is incapacitated, dies, resigns, or is for any reason unable to hold his office or is removed from office (impeached and convicted), people in the following offices will assume the office of the President in this order, provided they are qualified. The must be at least 35 years old, a natural-born U.S. citizen and have lived in the U.S. for at least 14 years.

- Vice President
- Speaker of the House
- President Pro Tempore of the Senate
- Secretary of State
- Secretary of the Treasury
- Secretary of Defense
- Attorney General
- Secretary of the Interior
- Secretary of Agriculture

- Secretary of Commerce
- Secretary of Labor
- Secretary of Health and Human Services
- Secretary of Housing and Urban Development
- Secretary of Transportation
- Secretary of Energy
- Secretary of Education
- Secretary of Veterans Affair
- Secretary of Homeland Security

The President's Cabinet

The Cabinet is a group of the President's closest and most trusted advisors. They meet at least once a week. The Cabinet includes the vice president, the heads of 15 Executive Branch departments and other government officials chosen by the President.

The 14 Secretaries from the executive departments and the Attorney General are nominated by the President. They must be confirmed by 51 votes of the Senate. Nominees cannot be a member of Congress nor hold any other elected office. They serve as long as the President is in office.

Secretary of State
Works with other countries

Secretary of the Treasury
Supervises the collection of taxes and printing of money

Secretary of Defense
Oversees the armed forces

Attorney General
Enforces the laws of the U.S. government

Secretary of the Interior
Protects natural resources and wildlife

Secretary of Agriculture
Ensures a healthy food supply and supports farmers

Secretary of Commerce
Promotes business and job opportunities for all Americans, responsible for copyrights, patents, and trademarks and oversees matters related to oceans, weather, and technology

Secretary of Labor
Oversees the interests of U.S. workers

Secretary of Health & Human Services
Oversees the government agencies responsible for people's health, medical research, disease prevention and assures safety of food and drugs through financial assistance to low income families

Secretary of Housing & Development
Oversees housing needs and focuses on community improvement and development

Secretary of Transportation
Oversees the nation's transportation system: highways, railroads, ports and air travel

Secretary of Energy
Researches and develops environmentally friendly energy systems

Secretary of Education
Establishes guidelines for American education and helps local communities meet the needs of their students

Secretary of Veterans Affairs
Operates programs for veterans and their families

Secretary of Homeland Security
Works to prevent terrorist attacks within the United States, reduce America's vulnerability to terrorism, and minimize the damage from potential attacks and natural disasters

Judicial Branch

The judicial branch of the federal government includes trial and appellate courts, including the U.S. Supreme Court, which is the highest court in the land. Courts decide arguments about the meaning of laws, how they are applied and whether they violate the Constitution.

One of the modern Supreme Court's primary functions is to decide cases challenging the Constitution. Supreme Court constitutional decisions can only be changed by another Supreme Court decision or amending the Constitution.

The Supreme Court has eight Justices and one Chief Justice. They are appointed by the President and must be approved by the Senate. Justices serve for life unless they resign, retire, or are impeached by the House and/or convicted by the Senate.

Federalist Government

The U.S. Constitution established a federal system of government in the newly formed United States of America. A federal system of government, also known as federalism, divides the powers of government between the national (federal) government and state and local governments. Under federalism, each level of government has sovereignty in some areas and shares powers in other areas. For example, both the federal and state governments have the power to levy taxes against their citizens, whereas only the federal government can declare war. Governments on both the national and state level are set up in a systematic structure of three branches to maintain a balance of power: the legislative to make laws; the judicial to interpret those laws; and the executive to enforce the laws.

IMPORTANT HISTORICAL DOCUMENTS

Many of our freedoms and responsibilities come from our founding documents and the constitutions of each state. Understanding these documents is essential to the functions of government, culture and society.

What is The Declaration of Independence?

The Declaration of Independence stated 27 specific reasons the British colonies of North America decided to create a new nation in July of 1776. This document established an identity for the 13 colonies as the United States of America and broke all ties with Great Britain.

The Declaration of Independence is important because it is our country's most cherished symbol of liberty and Thomas Jefferson's most enduring monument.

The Declaration of Independence

When in the Course of human events, it becomes necessary for one people to dissolve the political bands which have connected them with another, and to assume among the powers of the earth, the separate and equal station to which the Laws of Nature and of Nature's God entitle them, a decent respect to the opinions of mankind requires that they should declare the causes which impel them to the separation.

We hold these truths to be self-evident, that all men are created equal, that they are endowed by their Creator with certain unalienable Rights, that among these are Life, Liberty and the pursuit of Happiness. — That to secure these rights, Governments are instituted among Men, deriving their just powers from the consent of the governed, — That whenever any Form of Government becomes destructive of these ends, it is the Right of the People to alter or to abolish it, and to institute new Government, laying its foundation on such principles and organizing its powers in such form, as to them shall seem most likely to effect their Safety and Happiness. Prudence, indeed, will dictate that Governments long established should not be changed for light and transient causes; and accordingly all experience hath shewn, that mankind are more disposed to suffer, while evils are sufferable, than to right themselves by abolishing the forms to which they are accustomed. But when a long train of abuses and usurpations, pursuing invariably the same Object evinces a design to reduce them under absolute Despotism, it is their right, it is their duty, to throw off such Government, and to provide new Guards for their future security. —Such has been the patient sufferance of these Colonies; and such is now the necessity, which constrains them to alter their former Systems of Government. The history of the present King of Great Britain is a history of repeated injuries and usurpations, all having in direct object the establishment of an absolute Tyranny over these States. To prove this, let Facts be submitted to a candid world.

He has refused his Assent to Laws, the most wholesome and necessary for the public good.

He has forbidden his Governors to pass Laws of immediate and pressing importance, unless suspended in their operation till his Assent should be obtained; and when so suspended, he has utterly neglected to attend to them.

He has refused to pass other Laws for the accommodation of large districts of people, unless those people would relinquish the right of Representation in the Legislature, a right inestimable to them and formidable to tyrants only.

He has called together legislative bodies at places unusual, uncomfortable, and distant from the depository of their public Records, for the sole purpose of fatiguing them into compliance with his measures.

He has dissolved Representative Houses repeatedly, for opposing with manly firmness his invasions on the rights of the people.

He has refused for a long time, after such dissolutions, to cause others to be elected; whereby the Legislative powers, incapable of Annihilation, have returned to the People at large for their exercise; the State remaining in the mean time exposed to all the dangers of invasion from without, and convulsions within.

He has endeavoured to prevent the population of these States; for that purpose obstructing the Laws for Naturalization of Foreigners; refusing to pass others to encourage their migrations hither, and raising the conditions of new Appropriations of Lands.

He has obstructed the Administration of Justice, by refusing his Assent to Laws for establishing Judiciary powers.

He has made Judges dependent on his Will alone, for the tenure of their offices, and the amount and payment of their salaries.

He has erected a multitude of New Offices, and sent hither swarms of Officers to harass our people, and eat out their substance.

He has kept among us, in times of peace, Standing Armies without the Consent of our legislatures.

He has affected to render the Military independent of and superior to the Civil power.

He has combined with others to subject us to a jurisdiction foreign to our constitution, and unacknowledged by our laws; giving his Assent to their Acts of pretended Legislation:

For Quartering large bodies of armed troops among us:

For protecting them, by a mock Trial, from punishment for any Murders which they should commit on the Inhabitants of these States:

For cutting off our Trade with all parts of the world:

For imposing Taxes on us without our Consent:

For depriving us in many cases, of the benefits of Trial by Jury:

For transporting us beyond Seas to be tried for pretended offences

For abolishing the free System of English Laws in a neighbouring Province, establishing therein an Arbitrary government, and enlarging its Boundaries so as to render it at once an example and fit instrument for introducing the same absolute rule into these Colonies:

For taking away our Charters, abolishing our most valuable Laws, and altering fundamentally the Forms of our Governments:

For suspending our own Legislatures, and declaring themselves invested with power to legislate for us in all cases whatsoever.

He has abdicated Government here, by declaring us out of his Protection and waging War against us.

He has plundered our seas, ravaged our Coasts, burnt our towns, and destroyed the lives of our people.

He is at this time transporting large Armies of foreign Mercenaries to compleat the works of death, desolation and tyranny, already begun with circumstances of Cruelty & perfidy scarcely paralleled in the most barbarous ages, and totally unworthy the Head of a civilized nation.

He has constrained our fellow Citizens taken Captive on the high Seas to bear Arms against their Country, to become the executioners of their friends and Brethren, or to fall themselves by their Hands.

He has excited domestic insurrections amongst us, and has endeavoured to bring on the inhabitants of our frontiers, the merciless Indian Savages, whose known rule of warfare, is an undistinguished destruction of all ages, sexes and conditions.

What is the Constitution?

The Constitution sets up the structure of the U.S. Government into three branches and lists all the powers of government. Powers not assigned to the government are reserved for the states. It specifies that the United States will be a republic, with an elected President, a Congress consisting of a House of Representatives and a Senate, and a system of courts headed by the Supreme Court. It is comprised of a Preamble (introduction), the Articles (the main section) and Amendments (additions made after the original Constitution was completed). The Constitution is the basic and supreme law of the United States and provides important limitations on government to protect fundamental rights of its citizens.

The Preamble

We the people of the United States, in order to form a more perfect union, establish justice, insure domestic tranquility, provide for the common defense, promote the general welfare, and secure the blessings of liberty to ourselves and our posterity, do ordain and establish this Constitution for the United States of America.

Articles of the Constitution

Article 1 states that Congress has control over legislation. It also states that the Congress is to be divided into two parts, or chambers: the House of Representatives and the Senate.

The House of Representatives
- Elected by the people to 2-year terms
- Must be at least 25 years old

- Must be a citizen of the U.S.
- Must be a resident in the state where elected

The Senate

- Each state has 2 senators
- Senators serve 6-year terms
- 1/3 of senators are elected at a time
- Must be at least 30 years old
- Must be a citizen of the U.S. at least 9 years
- Must be a resident in the state that elects them
- The Vice President presides over the Senate and can only cast a vote in the event of a tie
- In his absence the President pro tempore presides
- After the House has voted to impeach, the Senate tries the cases. It takes 2/3 of the Senate to convict
- Tax bills originate in the House. After a bill passes the House and the Senate, it goes before the President who has 10 days to decide whether to sign it or veto it. If the President does nothing, the bill becomes law automatically

The Congress

- Collects taxes
- Regulates commerce
- Coins money
- Manages a postal system
- Declares war
- Creates a judicial system
- Maintains a military
- Makes laws necessary for carrying out the Constitution
- Approves all money to be spent by the government

Article 2

Executive Power vested in a President of the United States of America

The President

- Ensures that the nation's laws are carried out and enforced

- Serves a 4-year term
- Is formally elected by the electors of the Electoral College
- Must be at least 35 years old
- Must be a United States citizen, born in the United States
- Must be a resident of the country for at least 14 years
- Is succeeded by the Vice President should he die
- Has wide authority in the Executive Branch
- Serves as Commander in Chief of the Armed Forces
- Has the power to grant pardons in criminal cases
- Has supervisory responsibility in the Executive Branch departments
- Can be removed from office if convicted of commiting a serious offense. This applies to the Vice President and other top officials as well

Article 3
Judicial Power of the United States

- The Judicial power shall be vested in the Supreme Court.
- The Supreme Court has some control over the legal system.
- Supreme Court Justices hold their seats for life, unless they violate significant laws.
- Americans have the right to a jury trial.
- The trial must be held in the state in which the crime was allegedly committed.
- Persons accused of treason can only be punished if there are two witnesses to the crime, or if the person confesses in court.

Article 4
Full Faith and Credit

- States must accept most laws and legal decisions made by other states.
- States must offer to both nonresidents and residents of the state, most fundamental legal rights.
- People who commit serious crimes cannot seek refuge in other states.
- Congress controls the admission of new states.

- The government can use federal buildings, land, and property in any way it chooses.
- The government obligates itself to protect the states and to step in if needed for domestic problems.

Article 5

Proposing Amendments

- In order for an amendment to be passed, two-thirds of the states must call a Constitutional Convention to propose the amendment, which then must be passed by three-quarters of the states.
- Congress can propose amendments if two-thirds of the members in both chambers will vote to support it.
- After Congress proposes the Amendment, it takes three-quarters of the state legislatures to approve it.

Article 6

The Laws of the United States

- All laws made, whether federal, by each state, or locally must adhere to the laws set forth in the Constitution.
- All judges must hold the Constitution above any other law.
- All members of Congress, state legislatures, state and federal judges and state and federal executive officials must agree to support the Constitution.

Article 7

Ratification of the Conventions
- Only 9 of the original 13 states were needed to approve the Constitution.

What is The Bill of Rights?

The Bill of Rights, principally drafted by James Madison, is the first 10 amendments to the Constitution. It is a list of limits on government power.

The Bill of Rights

The Bill of Rights is the collective name for the first ten amendments to the United States Constitution, which limit the power of the U.S. federal government. These limitations serve to protect the natural rights of liberty and property including freedoms of religion, speech, a free press, free assembly, and free association, as well as the right to keep and bear arms.

Original Ten Amendments: The Bill of Rights

Passed by Congress September 25, 1789.
Ratified December 15, 1791.

Amendment I
> Freedoms, Petitions, Assembly

Congress shall make no law respecting an establishment of religion, or prohibiting the free exercise thereof; or abridging the freedom of speech, or of the press, or the right of the people peaceably to assemble, and to petition the Government for a redress of grievances.

Amendment II
> Right to bear arms

A well regulated Militia, being necessary to the security of a free State, the right of the people to keep and bear Arms, shall not be infringed.

Amendment III
Quartering of soldiers

No Soldier shall, in time of peace be quartered in any house, without the consent of the Owner, nor in time of war, but in a manner to be prescribed by law.

Amendment IV
Search and arrest

The right of the people to be secure in their persons, houses, papers, and effects, against unreasonable searches and seizures, shall not be violated, and no Warrants shall issue, but upon probable cause, supported by Oath or affirmation, and particularly describing the place to be searched, and the persons or things to be seized.

Amendment V
Rights in criminal cases

No person shall be held to answer for a capital, or otherwise infamous crime, unless on a presentment or indictment of a Grand Jury, except in cases arising in the land or naval forces, or in the Militia, when in actual service in time of War or public danger; nor shall any person be subject for the same offence to be twice put in jeopardy of life or limb, nor shall be compelled in any criminal case to be a witness against himself, nor be deprived of life, liberty, or property, without due process of law; nor shall private property be taken for
public use, without just compensation.

Amendment VI
Right to a fair trial

In all criminal prosecutions, the accused shall enjoy the right to a speedy and public trial, by an impartial jury of the State and district wherein the crime shall have been committed; which district shall have been previously ascertained by law, and to be informed of the nature and cause of the accusation; to be confronted with the witnesses against him; to have compulsory process for obtaining witnesses in his favor, and to have the assistance of counsel for his defence.

Amendment VII
> Rights in civil cases

In Suits at common law, where the value in controversy shall exceed twenty dollars, the right of trial by jury shall be preserved, and no fact tried by a jury shall be otherwise re-examined in any Court of the United States, than according to the rules of the common law.

Amendment VIII
> Bail, fines, punishment

Excessive bail shall not be required, nor excessive fines imposed, nor cruel and unusual punishments inflicted.

Amendment IX
> Rights retained by the People

The enumeration in the Constitution of certain rights shall not be construed to deny or disparage others retained by the people.

Amendment X
> States' rights

The powers not delegated to the United States by the Constitution, nor prohibited by it to the States, are reserved to the States respectively, or to the people.

Later Amendments

Amendment 11
Lawsuits against states

The Judicial power of the United States shall not be construed to extend to any suit in law or equity, commenced or prosecuted against one of the United States by Citizens of another State, or by Citizens or Subjects of any Foreign State.
February 7, 1795

Amendment 12
Presidential elections

The Electors shall meet in their respective states, and vote by ballot for President and Vice-President, one of whom, at least, shall not be an inhabitant of the same state with themselves; they shall name in their ballots the person voted for as President, and in distinct ballots the person voted for as Vice-President, and they shall make distinct lists of all persons voted for as President, and of all persons voted for as Vice-President, and of the number of votes for each, which lists they shall sign and certify, and transmit sealed to the seat of the government of the United States, directed to the President of the Senate;--The President of the Senate shall, in the presence of the Senate and House of Representatives, open all the certificates and the votes shall then be counted;--The person having the greatest number of votes for President, shall be the President, if such number be a majority of the whole number of Electors appointed; and if no person have such majority, then from the persons having the highest numbers not exceeding three on the list of those voted for as President, the House of Representatives shall choose immediately, by ballot, the President. But in choosing the President, the votes shall be taken by states, the representation from each state having one vote; a quorum for this purpose shall consist of a member or members from two-thirds of the states, and a majority of all the states shall be necessary to a choice. [And if the House of Representatives shall not choose a President whenever the right of choice shall devolve upon them, before the fourth day of March next following, then the Vice-President shall act as President, as in the case of the death or other constitutional disability of the President.]* The person having the greatest number of votes as Vice-President, shall be the Vice-President, if such number be a majority of the whole number of Electors appointed, and if no person have a majority, then from the two highest numbers on the list, the Senate shall choose the Vice-President; a quorum for the purpose shall consist of two-thirds of the whole number of Senators, and a majority of the whole number shall be necessary to a choice. But no person constitutionally ineligible to the office of President shall be eligible to that of Vice-President of the United States.

June 15, 1804 Superseded by Section 3 of the Twentieth Amendment.

Amendment 13
Abolition of slavery

Section 1. Neither slavery nor involuntary servitude, except as a punishment for crime whereof the party shall have been duly convicted, shall exist within the United States, or any place subject to their jurisdiction.

Section 2. Congress shall have power to enforce these article by appropriate legislation.

December 6, 1865

Amendment 14
Civil rights

Section 1. All persons born or naturalized in the United States and subject to the jurisdiction thereof, are citizens of the United States and of the State wherein they reside. No State shall make or enforce any law which shall abridge the privileges or immunities of citizens of the United States; nor shall any State deprive any person of life, liberty, or property, without due process of law; nor deny to any person within its jurisdiction the equal protection of the laws.

Section 2. Representatives shall be apportioned among the several States according to their respective numbers, counting the whole number of persons in each State, excluding Indians not taxed. But when the right to vote at any election for the choice of electors for President and Vice President of the United States, Representatives in Congress, the Executive and Judicial officers of a State, or the members of the Legislature thereof, is denied to any of the male inhabitants of such State, being twenty-one years of age, and citizens of the United States, or in any way abridged, except for participation in rebellion, or other crime, the basis of representation therein shall be reduced in the proportion which the number of such male citizens shall bear to the whole number of male citizens twenty-one years of age in such State.

Section 3. No person shall be a Senator or Representative in Congress, or elector of President and Vice President, or hold any office, civil or military, under the United States, or under any State, who, having previously taken an oath, as a member of Congress, or as an officer of the United States, or as a member of any State legislature, or as an executive or judicial officer of any State, to support the Constitution of the United States, shall have engaged in insurrection or rebellion against the same, or given aid or comfort to the enemies thereof. But Congress may by a vote of two-thirds of each House, remove such disability.

Section 4. The validity of the public debt of the United States, authorized by law, including debts incurred for payment of pensions and bounties for services in suppressing insurrection or rebellion, shall not be questioned. But neither the United States nor any State shall assume or pay any debt or obligation incurred in aid of insurrection or rebellion against the United States, or any claim for the loss or emancipation of any slave; but all such debts, obligations and claims shall be held illegal and void.

Section 5. The Congress shall have power to enforce, by appropriate legislation, the provisions of this article.
July 9, 1868

Amendment 15
Black suffrage

Section 1. The right of citizens of the United States to vote shall not be denied or abridged by the United States or by any State on account of race, color, or previous condition of servitude.

Section 2. The Congress shall have power to enforce this article by appropriate legislation.
February 3, 1870

Amendment 16
Income taxes

The Congress shall have power to lay and collect taxes on incomes, from whatever source derived, without apportionment among the several States, and without regard to any census or enumeration.
February 3, 1913

Amendment 17
Senatorial elections

The Senate of the United States shall be composed of two senators from each State, elected by the people thereof, for six years; and each Senator shall have one vote. The electors in each State shall have the qualifications requisite for electors of the most numerous branch of the State legislature.

When vacancies happen in the representation of any State in the Senate, the executive authority of such State shall issue writs of election to fill such vacancies: Provided, That the legislature of any State may empower the executive thereof to make temporary appointments until the people fill the vacancies by election as the legislature may direct. This amendment shall not be so construed as to affect the election or term of any Senator chosen before it becomes valid as part of the Constitution.
April 8, 1913

Amendment 18
Prohibition of liquor

Section 1. After one year from the ratification of this article, the manufacture, sale, or transportation of intoxicating liquors within, the importation thereof into, or the exportation thereof from the United States and all territory subject to the jurisdiction thereof for beverage purposes is hereby prohibited.

Section 2. The Congress and the several States shall have concurrent power to enforce this article by appropriate legislation.

Section 3. This article shall be inoperative unless it shall have been ratified as an amendment to the Constitution by the legislatures of the several States, as provided in the Constitution, within seven years from the date of the submission hereof to the States by the Congress.
January 16, 1919. Repealed by the Twenty-First, December 5, 1933

Amendment 19
Women's suffrage

The right of citizens of the United States to vote shall not be denied or abridged by the United States or by any States on account of sex.

Congress shall have power to enforce this article by appropriate legislation.
August 18, 1920

Amendment 20
Terms of office

Section 1. The terms of the President and Vice President shall end at noon the 20th day of January, and the terms of Senators and Representatives at noon on the 3d day of January, of the years in which such terms would have ended if this article had not been ratified; and the terms of their successors shall then begin.

Section 2. The Congress shall assemble at least once in every year, and such meeting shall begin at noon on the 3d day of January, unless they shall by law appoint a different day.

Section 3. If, at the time fixed for the beginning of the term of the President, the President elect shall have died, the Vice President elect shall become President. If a President shall not have been chosen before the time fixed for the beginning of his term, or if the President elect shall have failed to qualify, then the Vice President elect shall act as President until a President shall have qualified; and the Congress may by law provide for the case wherein neither a President elect nor a Vice President elect shall have qualified, declaring who shall then act as President, or the manner in which one who is to act shall be selected, and such person shall act accordingly until a President or Vice President shall have qualified.

Section 4. The Congress may by law provide for the case of the death of any of the persons from whom the House of Representatives may choose a President whenever the right of choice shall have devolved upon them, and for the case of the death of any of the persons from whom the Senate may choose a Vice President whenever the right of choice shall have devolved upon them.

Section 5. Sections 1 and 2 shall take effect on the 15th day of October following the ratification of this article.

Section 6. This article shall be inoperative unless it shall have been ratified as an amendment to the Constitution by the legislatures of three-fourths of the several States within seven years from the date of its submission.
January 23, 1933

Amendment 21
    Repeal of Prohibition

Section 1. The eighteenth article of amendment to the Constitution of the United States is hereby repealed.

Section 2. The transportation or importation into any State, Territory, or possession of the United States for delivery or use therein of intoxicating liquors, in violation of the laws thereof, is hereby prohibited.

Section 3. The article shall be inoperative unless it shall have been ratified as an amendment to the Constitution by conventions in the several States, as provided in the Constitution, within seven years from the date of the submission hereof to the States by the Congress.
December 5, 1933

Amendment 22
Term Limits for the Presidency

Section 1. No person shall be elected to the office of the President more than twice, and no person who has held the office of President, or acted as President, for more than two years of a term to which some other person was elected President shall be elected to the office of the President more than once. But this Article shall not apply to any person holding the office of President when this Article was proposed by the Congress, and shall not prevent any person who may be holding the office of President, or acting as President, during the term within which this Article becomes operative from holding the office of President or acting as President during the remainder of such term.

Section 2. This article shall be inoperative unless it shall have been ratified as an amendment to the Constitution by the legislatures of three-fourths of the several States within seven years from the date of its submission to the States by the Congress.
February 27, 1951

Amendment 23
Washington, D.C., suffrage

Section 1. The District constituting the seat of government of the United States shall appoint in such manner as the Congress may direct:

A number of electors of President and Vice President equal to the whole number of Senators and Representatives in Congress to which the District would be entitled if it were a state, but in no event more than the least populous State; they shall be in addition to those appointed by the States, but they shall be considered, for the purposes of the election of President and Vice President, to be electors appointed by a State; and they shall meet in the District and perform such duties as provided by the twelfth article of amendment.

Section 2. The Congress shall have power to enforce this article by appropriate legislation.
March 29, 1961

Amendment 24
>Abolition of poll taxes

Section 1. The right of citizens of the United States to vote in any primary or other election for President or Vice President, for electors for President or Vice President, or for Senator or Representative in Congress, shall not be denied or abridged by the United States or any State by reason of failure to pay any poll tax or other tax.

Section 2. The Congress shall have power to enforce this article by appropriate legislation.
January 23, 1964

Amendment 25
>Presidential succession

Section 1. In case of the removal of the President from office or of his death or resignation, the Vice President shall become President.

Section 2. Whenever there is a vacancy in the office of the Vice President, the President shall nominate a Vice President who shall take office upon confirmation by a majority vote of both Houses of Congress.

Section 3. Whenever the President transmits to the President pro tempore of the Senate and the Speaker of the House of Representatives his written declaration that he is unable to discharge the powers and duties of his office, and until he transmits to them a written declaration to the contrary, such powers and duties shall be discharged by the Vice President as Acting President.

Section 4. Whenever the Vice President and a majority of either the principal officers of the executive departments or of such other body as Congress may by law provide, transmit to the President pro tempore of the Senate and the Speaker of the House of Representatives their written declaration that the President is unable to discharge the powers and duties of his office, the Vice President shall immediately assume the powers and duties of the office as Acting President.

Thereafter, when the President transmits to the President pro tempore of the Senate and the Speaker of the House of Representatives his written declaration that no inability exists, he shall resume the powers and duties of his office unless the Vice President and a majority of either the principal officers of the executive department or of such other body as Congress may by law provide, transmit within four days to the President pro tempore of the Senate and the Speaker of the House of Representatives their written declaration that the President is unable to discharge the powers and duties of his office. Thereupon Congress shall decide the issue, assembling within forty-eight hours for that purpose if not in session. If the Congress, within twenty-one days after receipt of the latter written declaration, or, if Congress is not in session, within twenty-one days after Congress is required to assemble, determines by two-thirds vote of both Houses that the President is unable to discharge the powers and duties of his office, the Vice President shall continue to discharge the same as Acting President; otherwise, the President shall resume the powers and duties of his office.
February 10, 1967

Amendment 26

18-year-old suffrage

Section 1. The right of citizens of the United States, who are eighteen years of age or older, to vote shall not be denied or abridged by the United States or by any State on account of age.

Section 2. The Congress shall have power to enforce this article by appropriate legislation.
June 30, 1971

Amendment 27
>Congressional pay raises

No law, varying the compensation for the services of the Senators and Representatives, shall take effect, until an election of Representatives shall have intervened.

May 7, 1992. (Note: Congress submitted the text of this amendment as part of the proposed Bill of Rights on September 27, 1789. The Amendment was not ratified together with the first ten Amendments.)

The Gettysburg Address

Gettysburg, Pennsylvania
November 19, 1863

On June 1, 1865, Senator Charles Sumner commented on what is now considered the most famous speech by President Abraham Lincoln. In his eulogy on the slain president, he called it a "monumental act." He said Lincoln was mistaken that "the world will little note, nor long remember what we say here." Rather, the Bostonian remarked, "The world noted at once what he said, and will never cease to remember it. The battle itself was less important than the speech."

Four score and seven years ago our fathers brought forth on this continent, a new nation, conceived in Liberty, and dedicated to the proposition that all men are created equal.

Now we are engaged in a great civil war, testing whether that nation, or any nation so conceived and so dedicated, can long endure. We are met on a great battle-field of that war. We have come to dedicate a portion of that field, as a final resting place for those who here gave their lives that that nation might live. It is altogether fitting and proper that we should do this.

But, in a larger sense, we can not dedicate -- we can not consecrate -- we can not hallow -- this ground. The brave men, living and dead, who struggled here, have consecrated it, far above our poor power to add or detract. The world will little note, nor long remember what we say here, but it can never forget what they did here. It is for us the living, rather, to be dedicated here to the unfinished work which they who fought here have thus far so nobly advanced. It is rather for us to be here dedicated to the great task remaining before us -- that from these honored dead we take increased devotion to that cause for which they gave the last full measure of devotion -- that we here highly resolve that these dead shall not have died in vain -- that this nation, under God, shall have a new birth of freedom -- and that government of the people, by the people, for the people, shall not perish from the earth.

DID YOU KNOW...

- The Supreme Court is the most powerful court in the United States. Its decisions cannot be appealed to any other court.

- Federal judges, with a few exceptions, are appointed for life.

- Appointed by the President, federal judges are confirmed by the Senate and have their pay determined by Congress.

- The U.S. Supreme Court and the Federal Courts of Appeals do not use juries.

- Only Congress can declare war.

- The Bill of Rights is composed of the first ten amendments to the Constitution.

- The Senate confirms presidential appointments.

- The number of members of the House of Representatives is fixed at 435. In the Senate, each state is equally represented by two members (currently 100).

- The Vice President casts the tie-breaking vote in the Senate.

- The Speaker of the House is the highest-ranking Congressional officer specified in the Constitution.

- Congress can override a presidential veto with a two-thirds vote.

- The Attorney General is the highest-ranking law enforcement official in the United States.

Inspirational Stories of People Making a Difference

These are the stories of people from nine to ninety, making a difference –

Inspiring stories of citizens taking part in civic and political processes to improve their community; promoting and supporting the election process; holding grassroots events to directly communicate with legislators; meeting with congressional representatives on Capitol Hill to make the case for their goals; socially responsible projects; writing powerful and persuasive letters to elected officials.

Make A Difference Day is the most encompassing national day of helping others. Held annually on the fourth Saturday of October, millions of Americans are rallied into a single day of action to help change the world.

Loved Twice

Loved Twice is a non-profit organizations started by Lisa Klein of Oakland, California. The organization collects baby clothes and packs them into 10-pound boxes. On Make A Difference Day, 45 volunteers packed 400 pounds of clothes at a Lexus dealership in San Jose, California. These bundles, on top of 700 pounds delivered to a hospital, helped clothe 110 infants for a year. Lisa was inspired to start Loved Twice when collecting clothes for Hurricane Katrina victims.

Second-Graders Learn A Tender Lesson In Giving

AnnMarie Castrogiovanni and her fellow second-grade teachers honored the memory of Jack Perlungher. He attended The Morgan Center, a preschool for kids with cancer in Hicksville, New York. Make A Difference Day would have been Jack's 6th birthday. Ninety-three students at Ogden Elementary in Valley Stream, New York were asked to do good deeds in exchange for cash to benefit the preschool. They raised $1,300 to buy a laptop in honor of Jack's love of computers.

A Community Rallies Against Winter's Blast

On Make A Difference Day, the Dubuque (Iowa) Area Weatherization Challenge repaired and insulated 70 homes of elderly, disabled, and low-income residents. The 225 concerned citizens included executives, retirees, Scouts, casino employees, nuns and Mayor Roy Buol.

Newman's Own

Paul Newman was committed to helping make the world a better place. To carry on his philanthropic legacy, Newman's Own Foundation donates all net royalties and profits from Newman's Own products after taxes to charities worldwide. The Newman's Own Foundation has donated more than $300 million since 1982. On Make A Difference Day, they made numerous donations to worthy causes.

Girl Scouts develops character to make the world a better place.

Happy Birthday to You!

Everyone should feel special on his or her birthday, and for children who are homeless, birthdays sometimes pass without fanfare. Using this sentiment as her inspiration, Rachael Cinalli of *Girl Scout Troop 50451* set out to help children in the Family Homeless Center in Vero Beach, Florida celebrate their birthday and create great memories. Rachel created a monthly birthday party celebration at the center, complete with cake, ice cream, games and prizes for all who came. She went into the community for donated presents so that every child would receive a gift on their special day. Not only did Rachel conduct a year's worth of birthday parties, she also secured donations of cake mix and icing so that her project can continue into the future.

Angelica House

Service to community has been at the heart of Sarah Rountree's

Girl Scout experience with *Troop 10864*, and she has spent a lot of her free time helping the homeless. When she found out that there are few resources to help the homeless look for jobs, she took action. She created a computer room and developed a job resource book at Angelica House, in Pompano Beach, Florida which is a part of Catholic Charities. Sarah also made bookshelves and sewed curtains to make the room more comfortable and friendly for job seekers.

The Boy Scouts of America provides a program that trains in the responsibilities of participating citizenship.

Quick Thinking Boy Scouts Save A Young Boy's Life

On April 20, 2009, after school, Life Scout Brian Fee and Star Scout Dale Raar were walking along busy Oxford Road in New Hartford, New York. They witnessed a van striking a boy crossing a road. They immediately ran into a steady stream of traffic and, based on Red Cross and Boy Scout training, began evaluating the injuries of the boy, who was lying in the middle of the road. The victim was coughing up blood, a sign of internal bleeding, and began to twitch and struggle. They realized that moving him could result in further injury, so they called 911 and held his head and feet to stabilize him. They remained in the middle of the road disregarding traffic until the police and ambulance arrived. As a result of their actions, Jared Chontow survived.

One man can make a difference. He can inspire the generosity of corporate America and communities.

KaBOOM! Is Dedicated To Saving Play

Darell Hammond is CEO of KaBOOM!, the Washington, D.C.-based, national non-profit organization dedicated to helping to support building playgrounds in low-income communities across the U.S. He grew up with seven brothers and sisters at the Mooseheart Child City & School, a group home outside of Chicago. The experience at Mooseheart instilled in Darell the power of volunteerism and the importance of helping those less fortunate get a head start. He helped lead the start-up of City Year Chicago after attending college. In 1996, he started KaBOOM! after reading an article in the *Washington Post* about two children dying in an abandoned car while playing. Under Darell Hammond's leadership of KaBOOM!, more than $200 million has been raised; a million volunteers have been rallied; 2,000 playgrounds were constructed; and a movement for the child's right to play was inspired.

The Do Something Awards celebrate a generation of doers: young people (25 and under) who recognize the need to do something, believe in their

ability to get it done and then take action. Meet a few of the 2011 Do Something Awards Finalists:

The Real Food Challenge

David Schwartz grew up in a low-income, Providence, Rhode Island neighborhood where the school food was so bad that he and his friends would often go all day without eating and spend whatever little money they had on fast food after the last bell rang. When his family later moved to a nearby affluent suburb, he was shocked by the disparities between his two communities—how access to healthy foods in the inner city was so devastatingly low and the diabetes rates so high. David created The Real Food Challenge to shift $1 billion of college food purchases toward local, sustainable, humane and fair trade sources by 2020. To date, over 35,000 students have taken part, and David and his team have trained over 1,700 student leaders at over 300 schools, all working together to build a healthy, fair and green food economy.

The Thirst Project

Seth Maxwell was a 19-year-old acting student in Los Angeles when a brief meeting with a friend who'd just returned from Africa changed the course of his life forever. Upon learning that almost one billion people lack access to clean water and that water-borne illnesses account for more than 80% of all global disease, he gave up acting to focus on water education. The Thirst Project is a movement of young people who are raising awareness of and bringing solutions to the global water crisis. Combining outreach and water well implementation, The Thirst Project has completed 392 freshwater development projects across the globe and reached 200,000 American students with its eye-opening educational programs.

YALLA: Youth And Leaders Living Actively

Mark Kabban, of San Diego, California is familiar with the linguistic, financial and educational struggles that immigrants face because of his own family's experience coming to the United States from war-torn Lebanon. He realized the power of sports and education after earning a college athletic scholarship, and established YALLA to empower immigrant families and their children, using soccer and art to help them develop the knowledge and confidence to pursue their goals. In 2010 YALLA provided over 150 refugee children with soccer scholarships, in addition to offering tutoring programs and community service opportunities, providing a full-rounded holistic program for refugee youth and their families.

Move For Hunger

Adam Lowy's great-grandfather started a moving company over 90 years ago. In working with his family, Adam has seen firsthand the amount of food that people throw away when they move. He recognized the potential of this wasted food and founded Move for Hunger, which works with 130 moving companies across 32 states to strengthen our nation's food banks. The organization has collected to date 150,000 pounds of food for food banks.

Summaries of the Articles From *Insights on Law & Society*

*Published by the American Bar Association Division
for Public Education*

Future Civic Leaders Engage Young People

Future Civic Leaders (FCL) is a Washington, D.C., based non-profit organization founded by Allen Gannett. Through summer conferences and high school clubs around the country, students learn about the political process and the way our government works. FCL empowers students to take part in civic and political processes to improve their community.

Democracy: It's Up to Youth

Youth Leadership Initiative (YLI) at University of Virginia Center for Politics was founded to combat apathy and cynicism toward the political process in the United States. The organization created innovative programs that motivate educators and students to get involved in the political process and become active in promoting and supporting the election process.

Learning Through Leadership: The Youth for Justice National Teach-In

The National Teach-In project of Youth for Justice was started in 2003. Middle and high school students learn about democracy by teaching other students about important questions of liberty, security, justice and equality in America. Innovative methods are used to explain concepts: hand-made coloring books to teach about the Bill of Rights, writing and performing in plays based on Supreme Court cases, snooping in backpacks to demonstrate search and seizure procedures. There is a great takeaway from learning through teaching for the "student" teachers and their "pupils."

Horatio Alger Awards

The Horatio Alger Association of Distinguished Americans, Inc. bears the name of the renowned author Horatio Alger, Jr., whose tales of overcoming adversity through unyielding perseverance and basic moral principles captivated the public in the late 19th century. The Association, a 501c3 non-profit educational organization, was established in 1947 to dispel the mounting belief among the nation's youth that the American Dream was no longer attainable.

The Mikva Challenge: Students and Democracy

The Mikva Challenge is a Chicago-based organization founded in 1997. Their mission is encouraging young people to learn civics through actively participating in the democratic process. Students who wish to make a difference at the school, community, state, or federal level create civic action projects. Examples include: remodeling homeless shelters, introducing recycling ordinances in city councils and meeting with a police commander to talk about reducing violence. The Mikva Active Citizen Project has recruited and trained high school seniors to work in polling places on election day. These students influence family and friends to vote.

One of the Youngest American Patriots

Young American citizen Rohith Karthik began learning to read when he was two years old, so his parents enrolled him in math and English classes before he began pre-school. Karthikeyan Pancharcharam and HemaMalina Panchaksharam were surprised when they witnessed their son's memory skills at such an early age. He was able to recall dates of important family occasions without any reference other than memory. That motivated them to encourage him to read books on subjects that interested him. By age four, he took a special interest in learning everything he could about his country and its history. He became so proficient in his studies of American history and the American Presidents that by the time he was in kindergarten during the 2010-11 school year, he set out to encourage and inspire his classmates to also take an interest in learning about their country. Part of that effort was to write a children's book before he entered first grade that could be shared with children of all ages. That book, entitled "Hey Kids, America Needs Us!" was published by Star Books, the book division of StarGroup International, during the summer of 2011.

QUOTATIONS

And so, my fellow Americans: ask not what your country can do for you – ask what you can do for your country.

~John F. Kennedy

Every good citizen makes his country's honor his own, and cherishes it not only as precious but as sacred. He is willing to risk his life in its defense and is conscious that he gains protection while he gives it.

~Andrew Jackson

Citizenship comes first today in our crowded world ... No man can enjoy the privileges of education and thereafter with a clear conscience break his contract with society. To respect that contract is to be mature, to strengthen it is to be a good citizen, to do more than your share under it is noble.

~Isaiah Bowman

Citizenship consists in the service of the country.

~Jawaharlal Nehru

The best way to find yourself is to lose yourself in the service of others.

~Mohandas Gandhi

Like the body that is made of different limbs and organs, all moral creatures must depend on each other to exist.

~Anonymous

It is not the function of our Government to keep the citizen from falling into error; it is the function of the citizen to keep the Government from falling into error.

~Anonymous

We all have an obligation as citizens of this earth to leave the world a healthier, cleaner, and better place for our children and future generations.

~Blythe Danner

Voting is the least arduous of a citizen's duties. He has the prior and harder duty of making up his mind.

~Ralph Barton Perry

At this auspicious period, the United States came into existence as a Nation; and if their Citizens should not be completely free and happy, the fault will be entirely their own.

~George Washington

Bad officials are elected by good citizens who do not vote.

~George Jean Nathan

Let each citizen remember at the moment he is offering his vote that he is not making a present or a compliment to please an individual – or at least that he ought not to do so; but that he is executing one of the most solemn trusts in human society for which he is accountable to God and his country.

~Anonymous

I believe if a private citizen is able to affect public opinion in a constructive way he doesn't have to be an elected public servant to perform a public service.

~Warren Beatty

The first requisite of a good citizen in this republic of ours is that he shall be able and willing to pull his own weight.

~Theodore Roosevelt

Justice in the life and conduct of the State is possible only as first it resides in the hearts and souls of the citizens.

~Plato

Democracy is the government of the people, by the people, for the people.

~Abraham Lincoln

A good objective of leadership is to help those who are doing poorly to do well and to help those who are doing well to do even better.

~Jim Rohn

A kind and compassionate act is often its own reward.

~William John Bennett

As long as you derive inner help and comfort from anything, keep it.

~Mahatma Gandhi

Be charitable before wealth makes thee covetous.

~Sir Thomas Browne

Believe, when you are most unhappy, that there is something for you to do in the world. So long as you can sweeten another's pain, life is not in vain.

~Helen Keller

Blessed are those who can give without remembering and take without forgetting.

~Elizabeth Bibesco

Charity sees the need, not the cause.

~German Proverb

Every great man is always being helped by everybody; for his gift is to get good out of all things and all persons.

~John Ruskin

Everyone needs help from everyone.

~Bertolt Brecht

When a person is down in the world, an ounce of help is better than a pound of preaching.

~Edward G. Bulwerj-Lytton

Time and money spent in helping men do more for themselves is far better than mere giving.

~Henry Ford

Help your brother's boat across and your own will reach the shore.

~Hindu Proverb

In about the same degree that you are helpful, you will be happy.

~Karl Reiland

The race of mankind would perish did they cease to aid each other. We cannot exist without mutual help. All therefore that need aid have a right to ask it from their fellow-men; and no one who has the power of granting can refuse it without guilt.

~Sir Walter Scott

Generosity gives assistance, rather than advice.

~Vauvenargues

Provision for others is a fundamental responsibility of human life.

~Woodrow Wilson

The true value of a human being is determined by the measure and the sense in which they have obtained liberation from the self.

~Albert Einstein

Lost causes are the only ones worth fighting for.

~Clarence Darrow

The only reward of virtue is virtue; the only way to have a friend is to be one.
                          ~Ralph Waldo Emerson

It is one of the most beautiful compensations of life, that no man can sincerely try to help another without helping himself.
                          ~Ralph Waldo Emerson

A man wrapped up in himself makes a very small package.
                          ~Benjamin Franklin

Man may be defined as the animal that can say I, that can be aware of himself as a separate entity.
                          ~Erich Fromm

There are those who look at things the way they are, and ask why. I dream of things that never were, and ask why not?
                          ~Robert F. Kennedy

In the end, we will remember not the words of our enemies, but the silence of our friends.
                          ~Martin Luther King, Jr.

He has a right to criticize, who has a heart to help.
                          ~Abraham Lincoln

No man stands so tall as when he stoops to help a child.
                          ~Abraham Lincoln

The time is always right to do right
                          ~Nelson Mandella

Do not wait for leaders; do it alone, person to person.
                          ~Mother Theresa

Let no one ever come to you without leaving better and happier. Be the living expression of God's kindness.

~Mother Theresa

Necessity… is the mother of invention.

~Plato

No man is an Island, entire of itself…

~John Donne

It is amazing what you can accomplish if you do not care who gets the credit.

~Harry S. Truman

Nothing in the world can take the place of Persistence. Talent will not; nothing is more common than unsuccessful men with talent. Genius will not; unrewarded genius is almost a proverb. Education will not; the world is full of educated derelicts. Persistence and determination alone are omnipotent. The slogan 'Press On' has solved and always will solve the problems of the human race.

~Calvin Coolidge

HOW YOU CAN BE A BETTER AMERICAN CITIZEN

"We in America do not have government by the majority. We have government by the majority who participate."

~Thomas Jefferson

In America today, citizenship means, first and foremost, being recognized as a legal citizen of our country. But it is important that citizenship take on a deeper meaning. Citizens should actively work towards the betterment of their community through economic participation, public service, volunteer work and other such efforts to improve life for all citizens. Citizens should actively participate in the public life of a community in an informed, committed and constructive manner, with a focus on the common good. This is *civic* responsibility.

Only by engaging in civic responsibility – *being a better American citizen* - can we ensure the preservation of our democratic values as written in the U.S. Constitution and Bill of Rights. These values include justice, freedom, diversity, privacy, patriotism, rule of law, due process and tolerance.

"The success of the Republic is predicated upon the high individual efficiency of the average citizen."

~Theodore Roosevelt

Reasons To Be A Better American Citizen

The future of our country depends upon our active participation in keeping it strong.

If our democracy is weak, we become vulnerable to attack or financial crisis.

A nation, or a collection of nations, is really just the total of the lives of the people who comprise it. Make yours count.

When things aren't right, write a letter or an op-ed, join a march or make a donation.

Find ways to be part of the whole. We are a country of rugged individualists. When we work together we are a force to be reckoned with.

Appreciate the many freedoms and opportunities this country has to offer that are not found anyplace else in the world.

Our optimism, entrepreneurial spirit and willingness to adapt to changing conditions is a key strength of American people.

We live in a country where individual rights are respected.

In America, every citizen is entitled to the rights guaranteed by the Constitution, regardless of heritage, social standing or economic condition.

Every American has the right to peacefully assemble and speak his/her mind without fear.

Under U.S. law, a person is presumed innocent until proven guilty. No one is compelled to testify against himself, nor be deprived of life, liberty or property without due process of law.

Our American tradition is to rise above our own individual well-being to serve others in times of crisis or disaster.

The balance of powers, as guaranteed in our Constitution, prevents us from ever becoming a monarchy or a dictatorship, as can happen in other countries around the world.

Liberty is a way of life in our country, not a dream or a goal.

Higher civic engagement among teens correlates with greater academic achievement.

Political scientists and others who study the democratic process are finding that those skills and traits (associated with good citizenship) often correlate with… lower crime rates, higher academic achievement, the creation of jobs and improved health care delivery.

According to the Knight Foundation, there is a strong level of correlation between levels of civic engagement and cities' rates of economic growth.

America makes an ongoing effort to establish principles of civil liberties and civil rights throughout the world.

Each individual has the right to self-expression through art, literature, lifestyle or dress without fear of retribution.

American citizens are provided safe sanctuary in a U.S. embassy anywhere in the world.

Every registered citizen has the right to vote – regardless of race, color or gender.

The humblest and poorest of men and women can hold the highest privileges and positions, attaining these positions through merit and hard work.

Every citizen has the right to vote, regardless of race, color or gender.

There exists freedom of the press without government intervention or control.

Citizens have the right to petition the government to voice grievances – we are considered good and active citizens if we do so.

Our melting pot of cultural expressions based on a long history of welcoming immigrants seeking a better life in America provides an environment of innovation, diversity and collaboration.

Each person has the right to not worship or worship and practice whatever religion they choose, without threat of persecution.

Ways To Be A Better American Citizen

Say "thank you" to someone in the armed services. Show your appreciation for the sacrifices they make so that we can live in freedom.

Vote. Participate in the democratic process to elect officials who represent your point of view.

Help someone in need in your community. Serving a meal at a soup kitchen or donating canned goods to a food pantry are just two examples of how you can help people in your community.

Email or write to your mayor, congressman or President. Suggest ways to improve things in your community.

Join and actively participate in political parties.

Speak out. Each individual has the freedom of speech – the right to voice an opinion without fear of reprisal.

Willingly accept and perform jury duty.

Volunteer for military service and defend your country.

Enter public discussions or write letters to the editor about important current issues.

Join activist organizations and campaign for social causes.

Make financial contributions to political and social causes.

Be a good and helpful neighbor.

Stay informed about issues confronting society through diverse and credible sources.

Volunteer your special skills to an organization.

Donate blood.

Start a community garden.

Mentor someone of a different ethnic or religious group.

Help someone in need. Pay it forward.

Volunteer in your child's classroom or chaperone a field trip.

Participate in political campaigns.

Run for public office.

Serve on a town committee.

Read and understand the local news.

Attend a public meeting.

Help to build a neighborhood playground.

Respect and obey federal, state and local laws.

Respect the rights, beliefs and opinions of others.

Pay income and other taxes honestly, and on time, to federal, state and local authorities. Taxes fund social programs, the military, Social Security, welfare and education.

Learn the names of your congressmen and women, the representatives in the state assembly and the Senate.

Give a *service* to your neighbor, family, friend, or even a stranger.

Help preserve the planet: recycle, reduce air pollution, preserve natural resources, conserve water.

Participate in the government process. Voting is the most important and direct way to be involved.

Stay informed. Informed citizens are more adept at participating and responding to local and national affairs. Keep up to date on contemporary events and affairs by reading newspapers and news magazines, listening to news broadcasts on the radio, television and using the internet.

Have faith in yourself that you have the power to change your life and make it better.

Have a sense of history. This helps to understand and evaluate the contemporary political world.

Volunteer in your community. Offer your time by visiting senior citizen centers, volunteering at local hospitals, coaching children's sports teams and engaging in community improvement projects.

Show respect to the American flag. When saying the pledge, stand with the right hand over the heart or at attention. Men remove their hats. Military personnel and veterans give the military salute.

Attend public forums. Local and city governments encourage civic participation in public forums. There you can air grievances, offer suggestions and engage in public debate with local government officials and fellow citizens. Take the opportunity to make your voice heard.

Show compassion to people on a daily basis. Being compassionate and attentive to the needs of others is one of the most practical and valuable ways to practice good citizenship.

Join a civic organization such as Rotary International, Kiwanis International or Chamber of Commerce. Show pride and take responsibility for the community in which you live.

VOLUNTEERING

Volunteering is helping others in need without
monetary compensation for time or services.
Volunteers provide their time, skills or financial support
to organizations which promote good causes or
improve the quality of life for people in the community.
The primary purpose of volunteering is to help others.
Additional benefits include meeting new people,
learning new skills and having fun.

Volunteer opportunities are available for many causes. Some require a particular skill or talent, such as providing medical help through Doctors Without Borders or building homes with Habitat for Humanity; and some require only time and effort, such as walking dogs at the Humane Society.

Helping others in need is an important part of the American way of life. According to the Corporation for National and Community Service, 63.4 million Americans of all ages and backgrounds volunteered to help their communities in 2009, contributing 8.1 billion hours of service.

With the help of volunteers, changes in the world that seem impossible can become possible.

A few different types of volunteer opportunities are:

Community Volunteering – Help local community organizations to impact the lives of friends and neighbors. Support understaffed neighborhood, religious groups or local schools.

Corporate Volunteering – Volunteering on company time is encouraged by many Fortune 500 companies. This strengthens the company's sense of social responsibility as well as builds a sense of community among the employees.

Virtual Volunteering – There is a new opportunity for those who have limited time, or live far from a volunteering location. Volunteers work from home computers, smart phones or other internet-connected devices to provide valuable services. This is referred to as e-volunteering, cyber service, telementoring or teletutoring.

School Volunteering – Provide assistance to overworked teachers and staff members.

Environmental Volunteering – Help the environment by recycling, teaching others to recycle, community gardening or cleaning up beaches or neighborhoods.

Disaster Relief Volunteering - After a disaster, assist organizations that provide food, shelter, cleaning supplies, comfort kits, first aid, clothing, emergency transportation, home repairs, household items and medical supplies to victims.

SERVICE-LEARNING

Service-learning is a powerful educational tool that combines classroom learning with important community service. "Learning by doing" enables students from kindergarten to college to channel academic and critical thinking skills into meeting genuine community needs. Community involvement outside of the classroom contributes significantly to what students learn within class and helps students develop into socially responsible adults.

If a student group implements a recycling program in their school, that is *community service*. If the student group adds to that an analysis of the recycling program's impact on the school's carbon footprint, and then educates the rest of the school community on the environmental and financial benefits achieved by the recycling program – that is *service-learning*.

A national study of *Learn and Serve America* programs suggests that effective service-learning programs improve grades, increase attendance

in school, and develop students' personal and social responsibility.
Whether the goal is academic improvement, personal development or both, service-learning can help students learn critical thinking, communication, teamwork, civic responsibility, mathematical reasoning, problem solving, public speaking, vocational skills, computer skills, scientific method, research skills and analysis. Service-learning is a win-win situation: our students learn, and our communities are served.

THE PLEDGE OF ALLEGIANCE

The Youth's Companion, a weekly magazine for children in the 1880s, included adventure stories. In 1888 it published a special project asking children to help buy flags for their schools. Students collected enough money to buy 30,000 flags.

In 1892, two men from *The Youth's Companion,* Francis Bellamy and James Upton, wanted to celebrate the 400th anniversary of the arrival of Christopher Columbus. The men proposed that the children raise their new American flags at their schools and say something in its honor.

Bellamy went to Washington, D.C. where he shared the idea with President Benjamin Harrison. The President liked the plan, and Columbus Day was born.

In August 1892, Bellamy penned the famous words that became the Pledge of Allegiance:

I pledge allegiance to my Flag

and to the Republic for which it stands –

one Nation indivisible –

with liberty and justice for all.

The pledge was printed in *The Youth's Companion,* and teachers across America helped their students learn the meaning of the words.

Pledge is a promise.

Allegiance means to love and be true to something.

Republic is the government of the United States.

Nation means country.

Indivisible means that something cannot be divided or pulled apart.

Liberty means freedom.

Justice means being fair, having the same laws for all people.

In 1923 the words "The flag of the United States of America" were added. In 1954, an amendment was made to add the words "under God."

I pledge allegiance to the flag

of the United States of America

and to the Republic for which it stands,

one Nation under God, indivisible,

with liberty and justice for all.

THE AMERICAN ARMED FORCES

The armed forces are the protectors of the nation.

(The numbers for the Armed Services are continuosuly changing)

The Army

The Army is a powerful military force of 69,000 officers, 11,500 warrant officers and 450,000 enlisted soldiers working in many types of jobs, from general administration to the operation and maintenance of weapons, vehicles, aircraft, and highly technical electronic systems.

Soldiers, working as a team, perform the Army's mission of protecting the security of the United States and its vital resources. The Army stands ready to defend the interests of America and its allies through land-based operations anywhere in the world.

The Navy

The Navy is made up of about 400,000 officers and enlisted people who operate and repair more than 340 ships and over 4,000 aircraft. Some of the jobs include communications specialists, computer programmers and ship electricians. Navy personnel serve on ships, submarines, in aviation jobs on land and sea, and at shore bases around the world. The Navy helps maintain the freedom of the seas. It defends the right of America and its allies to travel and trade freely on the oceans of the world and helps protect the country during times of international conflict.

The Marine Corps

The Marine Corps, one of the most elite fighting forces in the world, is part of the Department of the Navy and operates in close cooperation with U.S. Naval forces at sea. Marines serve on U.S. Navy ships, protect Naval bases, guard U.S. embassies, and provide quick strike force to protect U.S. interests around the world. To perform the many duties of the Marine Corps, approximately 174,000 officers and enlisted Marines fly planes and helicopters, operate radar equipment, drive armored vehicles, gather intelligence, survey and map territory, maintain and repair radios, computers, jeeps, trucks, tanks, and aircraft, and perform hundreds of other challenging jobs.

The Air Force

The Army Air Corps was part of the U.S. Army during World War II. Toward the end of the war it was established as a separate branch of the armed forces and called the U.S. Air Force. The Air Force is the primary aerospace arm of America's armed forces. The men and women of the Air Force fly, maintain and support the world's most technically advanced aerospace vehicles, including long-range bombers, supersonic fighters, Airborne Warning and Control System (AWACS) aircraft and many others. These forces are used whenever and wherever necessary to protect our country and its allies.

The Air Force is made up of nearly 385,000 men and women, including 76,000 officers who pilot multi-million dollar aircraft, launch satellites, gather sensitive intelligence data, manage maintenance and more.

The Coast Guard

The Coast Guard is a part of the U.S. Department of Transportation and is the smallest of the armed services. The Coast Guard's most visible job is saving lives and property in and around American waters. The Coast Guard enforces customs and fishing laws, protects marine wildlife, fights pollution on the lakes and along the American coastline and conducts the International Ice Patrol. It is also responsible for monitoring traffic in major harbors, keeping shipping lanes open on ice-bound lakes and maintaining lighthouses and other navigation aides. In time of war it may be placed under the command of the Department of the Navy. An important part of the armed services, the Coast Guard has participated in every major American military campaign. There are 5,864 commissioned officers, 1,520 warrant officers, and 29,839 enlisted members.

The National Guard

When the National Guard's oldest regiments met for their first drill on the village green in Salem, Massachusetts, they were barely three months old. Organized on December 13, 1636, we now celebrate that date as the National Guard birthday.

In 1637, the English settlements in North America were a tiny fringe along the Eastern seaboard. As settlement pushed west into the interior, the institution of the militia, which the colonists brought with them from England, went with them.

The militia tradition meant citizens organizing themselves into military units, responsible for their own defense. Organizing the militia into regiments increased its efficiency and responsiveness, which proved critical for the defense of their communities. Its oldest units are among the oldest military units in the world.

What were formerly identified as state militias became the National Guard in 1916, serving communities, states, and the nation for nearly 400 years. Citizen-soldiers have fought in every major American conflict from 1637 to present day operations in Afghanistan and Iraq. Much has changed since the "first muster," but more than 370 years later, the men and women of the National Guard are still defending their neighbors – and their nation.

AMERICAN HOLIDAYS

New Year's Day

Celebrates the beginning of a new calendar year

January 1

Martin Luther King, Jr. Day

Celebrates the birth of slain civil rights leader

Third Monday in January

Presidents' Day

Honors all American Presidents, especially George Washington
and Abraham Lincoln

Third Monday in February

Professional Secretaries Day

Honors secretaries who have helped all businesses

Fourth Wednesday in April

Law Day

Commemorated since 1958 to mark America's commitment
to the rule of law

May 1

Mother's Day

This day was first celebrated in 1907 in Philadelphia, Pennsylvania to
honor all mothers. At this observance, Anna Jarvis asked her church
to have a special service on the day of her mother's death

Second Sunday in May

Armed Forces Day

Established in 1950 to honor our armed forces

Third Saturday in May

Memorial Day

Honors the dead, especially those who were killed in wars

Last Monday in May

Flag Day

On this date in 1777, Congress declared that the Stars & Stripes flag
would be the national flag of the United States

June 14

Father's Day

This day was first celebrated in Spokane, Washington on June 19,
1910. It was declared a national holiday in 1966

Third Sunday in June

Independence Day

Celebrates the date our country became independent
from Great Britain
July 4

Labor Day

Honors working people and labor unions

First Monday in September

Constitution Day

Celebrates the drafting of the United States Constitution

September 17

Columbus Day

Celebrates Christopher Columbus' arrival in America

Second Monday in October

National Boss Day

A day to show your boss he/she is appreciated

October 16

United Nations Day

Celebrates the founding of the United Nations in 1945

October 24

Election Day

This is the day a national election is held. The national elections are usually held in the even numbered years

First Tuesday in November

Veterans Day

Honors soldiers of all wars and commemorates the signing of the Armistice ending World War I in 1918

November 11

Thanksgiving Day

A day to give thanks for the harvest and all of our blessings

Fourth Thursday in November

PRESIDENTS &
VICE PRESIDENTS

Presidents		Vice Presidents
George Washington	1789-1797	John Adams
John Adams	1797-1801	Thomas Jefferson
Thomas Jefferson	1801-1809	Aaron Burr, George Clinton
James Madison	1809-1817	George Clinton, Eldridge Gerry
James Monroe	1817-1825	Daniels D. Tompkins
John Quincy Adams	1825-1829	John C. Calhoun
Andrew Jackson	1829-1837	Martin Van Buren
Martin Van Buren Johnson	1837-1841	Richard Mentor
William Henry Harrison	1841	John Tyler
John Tyler	1841-1845	None
James Knox Polk	1845-1849	George Mifflin Dallas

Presidents		Vice Presidents
Zachary Taylor	1849-1850	Millard Fillmore
Millard Fillmore	1850-1853	
Franklin Pierce	1853-1857	William Rufus King
James Buchanan	1857-1861	John C. Breckinridge
Abraham Lincoln	1861-1865	Hannibal Hamlin, Andrew Johnson
Andrew Johnson	1865-1869	None
Ulysses Simpson Grant	1869-1877	Schuyler Colfax, Henry Wilson
Rutherford B.Hayes	1877-1881	Schuyler Colfax, Henry Wilson
James Abram Garfield	1881	Chester Alan Arthur
Chester Alan Arthur	1881-1885	None
Grover Cleveland	1885-1889	Thomas Hendricks
Benjamin Harrison	1889-1893	Levi Parsons Morton
Grover Cleveland	1893-1897	Adlai E. Stevenson
William McKinley	1897-1901	Garret A. Hobart, Theodore Roosevelt
Theodore Roosevelt	1901-1909	Charles W. Fairbanks
William Howard Taft	1909-1913	James S. Sherman
Woodrow Wilson	1913-1921	Thomas R. Marshall
Warren G.Harding	1921-1923	Calvin Coolidge
Calvin Coolidge	1923-1929	Charles G. Dawes
Herbert Clark Hoover	1929-1933	Charles Curtis

Presidents		Vice Presidents
Franklin D. Roosevelt	1933-1945	John Nance Garner Henry A. Wallace Harry S. Truman
Harry S. Truman	1945-1953	Alben W. Barkley
Dwight D. Eisenhower	1953-1961	Richard M. Nixon
John F. Kennedy	1961-1963	Lyndon B. Johnson
Lyndon B. Johnson	1963-1969	Hubert H. Humphrey
Richard M. Nixon	1969-1974	Spiro T. Agnew Gerald R. Ford
Gerald R. Ford	1974-1977	Nelson A. Rockefeller
James E. Carter, Jr.	1977-1981	Walter F. Mondale
Ronald W. Reagan	1981-1989	George H.W. Bush
George H.W. Bush	1989-1993	Dan Quayle
William J. Clinton	1993-2001	Albert Gore
George W. Bush	2001-2009	Richard Cheney
Barack Obama	2009-	Joseph Biden

GLOSSARY

Allegiance – Loyalty to a nation. The Pledge of Allegiance promises loyalty to the United States.

Allies – Countries that work together toward a common goal.

American - Any person or characteristic relating to the United States, its culture, government or history. It also refers to anyone who is a citizen of America, first discovered by the Italian explorer, Amerigo Vespucci.

Ambassador – A person who officially represents a country somewhere outside that country.

Abroad – Outside of one's home country; in a foreign country.

Bill – Legislation that has formally been introduced in Congress.

Capitalism – An economic system based on the values of a free market.

Citizen – Someone who by birth or naturalization owes loyalty to a country and is protected by it.

Citizenship – Taking an active role to improve one's country or community through participation in government, public service, advocacy or other actions which improve life for all citizens.

Civic responsibility – Participating in the public life of a community with a focus on the common good.

Civil rights – Idea that all people of a nation or society should be treated equally.

Congress – The legislative branch of the federal government that makes the laws. Congress is comprised of the House of Representatives and the Senate.

Constituents – People who are represented by an elected official.

Constitution – The document that explains how America's government is organized, what its powers are and how it works.

Declaration of Independence – The document that announced that the 13 original colonies were no longer under British rule and were now independent states. It was written mainly by Thomas Jefferson and adopted by the colonies on July 4, 1776.

Democracy – a political system in which a country's citizens rule through whatever form of government they choose to establish. Elected officials are expected to reflect the known or established views of their constituents, even if it means setting their own political views aside.

Democratic – 1. Having to do with government by the people or the idea of political equality for all. 2. One of 2 major political parties in the U.S.

Emancipation Proclamation – An order issued by President Abraham Lincoln during the Civil War to free slaves in the 11 confederate states.

Equality – The idea that all humans have the same rights, and that none are worse or lower than others simply because of their skin color or ethnic background.

Federal – Having to do with the national, or central, government, rather than the government of a specific state.

Federalism – A system of government that divides the powers of government between national (federal) and state and local governments.

Form N-400 – The application for naturalization.

Governor – The elected head of a state.

House of Representatives – Part of Congress, made up of 435 elected representatives who serve 2-year terms. The state's population determines the number of representatives the state has in the House.

Immigrant – Someone who leaves one country to live in another.

Independence Day – The holiday celebrating America's independence from England, celebrated each year on July 4th.

Judicial Branch – The part of the government that interprets the Constitution. It is made up of the court system, including the Supreme Court.

Justice – Fairness. A system of law where everybody receives fair and equal treatment from the system.

Legislative Branch – The part of the government that makes laws. It includes the Senate and the House of Representatives.

Liberties – Rights and freedoms.

Native Americans – People who were already living in America when the colonists landed.

Naturalization – The way a foreign-born person becomes a citizen of the United States.

Naturalization oath ceremony – Once the application for citizenship is accepted, the oath of allegiance is said in order to become a United States citizen.

Oath – A promise or vow; a pledge. In the oath of allegiance to the United States, there is a promise to renounce foreign allegiances, support the Constitution and serve the United States.

Passport – An official government document that proves citizenship and allows travel to other countries.

Patriotism – The act of loving, supporting, and defending one's country.

Ratification – To give formal consent to; when a majority of the state legislatures approve a proposed constitutional amendment.

Republic – The U.S. form of government, in which people rule by delegating the power to govern on their behalf to elected representatives and officials. These representatives are expected to act on their own best judgment to satisfy the needs and interests of the country

Republican – 1. When a country's political power comes from the citizens, not the rulers, and is put into use by representatives elected by the citizens. 2. One of 2 major political parties in the U.S.

Rights – Freedoms and privileges that people are fundamentally entitled to.

Rule of Law – A legal maxim that provides that no person is above the law, that no one can be punished by the state except for a breach of the law, and that no one can be convicted of breaching the law except in the manner set forth by the law itself. The rule of law stands in contrast to the idea that the leader is above the law, a feature of Roman law, Nazi law, and certain other legal systems

Senate – The part of Congress made up of 100 Senators (2 from each state) who serve six-year terms.

Speaker of the House – Leader of the House of Representatives who becomes President if both the President and Vice President cannot complete their terms.

Socialism – An economic system in which there is no private ownership, and all production and distribution of goods and services is shared equally among the population.

Supreme Court – The highest court in the United States. It is made up of 9 justices, including the Chief Justice, who are appointed by the President to lifetime terms.

Term limits – A limit on the number of terms that a leader can be elected to serve. A term is the length of time that a government leader serves before he or she must be elected once again.

United Nations – A group of countries that came together after World War II to try to prevent more wars and give aid to poorer countries.

Veto – The President's power to refuse to sign a bill into law.

Resource: http://www.ait.org.tw/infousa/enus/government/overview/docs/M-638.pdf

FACTS ABOUT AMERICA

Geography

World's third largest country by size after Canada and Russia
18.01 % of land is suitable for agriculture

Population

World's third largest country by population after China and India

Over 313 million (July 2011 estimate)

13.1 % aged 65 and over

Median Age: 36.9 years

82% of the population lives in cities

Life Expectancy: 78.37 years (ranked 50 in the world)

Ethnic Groups

White:	63.7 %
Hispanic or Latino:	16.3 %
Black or African-American:	12.2 %
American Indian/Alaska Native:	.7 %
Asian:	4.7 %
Hawaiian / Pacific Islander:	0.2 %
Some Other Race:.	2 %
Two or More Races:	2.0 %

Religions

Protestant:	51.3 %
Roman Catholic:	23.9 %
Mormon:	1.7 %
Jewish:	1.7 %
Other Christian:	1.6 %
Buddhist:.	7 %
Muslim:.	6 %
Unaffiliated:	12.1 %
None:	4.0 %

Languages

English:	82.1 %
Spanish:	10.7 %
Other Indo-European:	3.8 %
Asian & Pacific Island:	2.7 %
Other:	7 %

Communications

Land Line Telephones:	141 million
Cellular Telephones:	286 million

Resource: www.cia.gov/library/publications/theworld

• There are five U.S. states with no sales tax. They are: Alaska, Delaware, Montana, New Hampshire and Oregon.

• On an American $1 bill, there is an owl in the upper left-hand corner of the "1" encased in the "shield" and a spider hidden in the front upper right-hand corner.

• The U.S. flag has 50 stars representing the 50 states, and 13 stripes representing the 13 original colonies.

• Some U.S. cities have the same name as U.S. states.

These are:

Delaware, Arkansas
California, Maryland
Oregon, Wisconsin
Wyoming, Ohio
Indiana, Pennsylvania
Nevada, Missouri
Louisiana, Missouri
Kansas, Oklahoma
Michigan, North Dakota
Florida, Massachusetts

Resource: http://www.theholidayspot.com

• Barbara Bush is both wife and mother to a U.S. President. She is also a distant cousin of President Franklin Pierce. She is the only woman who was ever mother, wife, and cousin to a President.

• The first woman to run for President was Victoria Woodhull in 1872. Her running mate was Frederick Douglass. She was declared ineligible, but not because she was a woman. She would not yet be 35 years old until September after the January Inauguration Day. She received some votes, but they are not recorded in the official results.

• The first person to become President who was born in a hospital was Jimmy Carter.

Resource: http://www.squidoo.com/unitedstatesfun

• The "largest" city in the United States is Juneau, Alaska. It covers about 3,000 square miles. That's larger than the state of Delaware. Jacksonville, Florida is the largest city in the lower 48 states at just over 800 square miles.

• In 1954 General Motors became the first corporation in the U.S. to have $1 billion in net income.

• The most crooked street in the world is Snake Alley, located in Burlington, Iowa.

- Iced tea was first served at the 1904 St. Louis World's Fair. A British businessman wanted to increase tea sales in America.

- The first coast-to-coast telephone line was established in 1914.

- The London Bridge, built about 160 years ago in London, was transplanted in 1968 to Lake Havasu, Arizona.

- New York City was the first home of the country's first 150 television sets in 1936. The first program NBC broadcast was a cartoon of *Felix The Cat!*

- The Parthenon in Nashville, Tennessee is the world's only reproduction of the Parthenon in Athens, Greece.

- The oldest capital city in the U.S. is Santa Fe, New Mexico founded in 1610.

- The 33rd President was Harry S. Truman. What is his middle name? His parents were going to give him the name Shippe or Solomon, the names of his grandfathers. They could not agree, so they gave him just an initial, "S."

- American Indians were not made citizens of the U.S. until Congress acted in 1924.

- The tomato was put "on trial" on September 25, 1820 in Salem, New Jersey. In front of a courthouse, Robert Johnson ate a basket of tomatoes to prove they were not poisonous. The crowd waited for him to keel over dead. He didn't.

- The streets in Virginia City, Nevada were once unknowingly paved with silver ore. When the locals found out what it was, they tore up the streets in less than 2 days.

- President Barack Obama is listed as our 44th President, but only 43 men have held the office. Why? Grover Cleveland held office during two nonconsecutive terms. He was our 22nd and 24th President. Incidentally, his full name is Stephen Grover Cleveland.

- John Adams and Thomas Jefferson both died on July 4, 1826. This was 50 years to the day after the signing of the Declaration of Independence.

Resource: http://teachersindex.com/

- There wasn't a single pony in the Pony Express, just horses.
- America once issued a 5-cent bill during the Civil War to combat the coin shortage at the time.

Resource: http://www.funny2.com/facts.htm

- There were actually seven Presidents before George Washington, known historically as the "Presidents under the Articles of Confederation," with the official title of "President of the United States in Congress Assembled":

  1. John Hanson (1781-82)

  2. Elias Boudinot (1783)

  3. Thomas Mifflin (1784)

  4. Richard Henry Lee (1785)

  5. Nathan Gorman (1786)

  6. Arthur St. Clair (1787)

  7. Cyrus Griffin (1788)

- Thomas Jefferson's (1801-1809) Vice President, Aaron Burr, the first Vice President chosen by the House, was dropped from the ticket and later arrested for treason and murder.
- There was one individual who served in the position of President without ever being sworn in. March 4, 1849 the day the new President, Zachary Taylor (1849-50), would have taken office, fell on a Sunday. President James Polk left on schedule, but Taylor did not take the oath until the next day., so Missourian David Rice Atchinson, President Pro Tempore of the Senate, "held down the fort," taking no action until Taylor was sworn in.
- James Madison (1809-1827) was the smallest of all the Presidents. He was only 5'4" tall and weighed less than 100 pounds.
- The White House was painted white the year James Monroe (1817-1825) became President.
- John Quincy Adams (1825-1829) was the first President to have

his photo taken (April 13, 1843).

• Andrew Jackson's (1829-1837) wife, Rachel, smoked a pipe.

• Martin Van Buren (1837-1841) was the first President who was born a U.S. citizen.

• James K. Polk (1845-1849) was the only President in American history who managed to keep all of his campaign promises during his tenure. During the 1844 campaign, he made 5 promises: to acquire California from Mexico, to settle the Oregon dispute, to lower the tariff, to establish a sub-treasury, and to retire from the office after 4 years. When he left office, his campaign promises had all been fulfilled.

• Abraham Lincoln (1861-65) grew a beard because a little girl wrote him a letter telling him that he would look more handsome with a beard. He was once called two-faced by a rival, to which Lincoln responded, "If I had another face, do you think I'd wear this one?"

• Franklin Pierce (1853-1857) was the first President to have a Christmas tree in the White House.

• When John Wilkes Booth leaped onto the stage after shooting President Lincoln, he tripped on the American flag.

• When he died, Andrew Johnson (1865-1869) was buried wrapped in a U.S. flag with his well-worn copy of the Constitution under his head.

• The first blacks to enter Congress were elected in 1869 as members of the Republican Party, a trend that continued until the first black Democrat was elected in 1935.

• Ulysses S. Grant (1869-1877) was once arrested for speeding in his horse carriage while serving as President of the United States.

• Democrat Samuel Jones Tilden of New York won the presidential election of 1876, but a 15-member panel overturned the decision in favor of Republican candidate Rutherford B. Hayes (1877-1881) by the margin of one electoral vote. Hayes' wife, Lucy, was the first President's wife to be called First Lady.

• James Garfield (1881) was the only man in U.S. history who was a congressman, senator-elect, and a President-elect at the same time. He campaigned for the presidency from the front porch of his house. He was also the last person to be elected to the presidency directly from the House of Representatives.

• Grover Cleveland (1885-1889) was the only President to serve two nonconsecutive terms in office. He was elected President in 1884, voted out of office in 1888, and was voted back in 1892.

• "Big Bill" William Howard Taft (1909-1913) was 6'2" and weighed over 300 pounds. On his Inauguration Day and weighing in at 340 pounds, he got stuck in the bathtub and had to be pried out by attendants.

• In 1912, Woodrow Wilson (1913-1921) defeated two Presidents in one election, incumbent President William Howard Taft, and former President Theodore Roosevelt.

• Laura Clay was the first woman to receive a vote for either President or Vice President at the 1920 Democratic National Convention in San Francisco.

• A man of few words, Calvin Coolidge (1923-1929) was famous for saying so little that a White House dinner guest made a bet that she could get the President to say more than two words. She told the President of her wager to which he replied, "You lose."

• Maine Senator Margaret Chase Smith was the first woman to receive a vote for the presidential nomination at a Republican National Convention.

• Both the Republican and Democratic National Conventions took place at the same time in Miami Beach in 1972.

• Gerald Ford was the only man who held both the presidency (1974-1977) and the vice-presidency (1973-1974) but who was not elected to either post.

• Three American Presidents attended a U.S. military academy. Dwight D. Eisenhower (1953-1961) and Ulysses S. Grant (1869-1877) both graduated from West Point; and Jimmy Carter (1977-1981) attended Annapolis.

• Ronald Reagan (1981-1989), at age 70, was the oldest person ever elected President, was the only divorced President, the only President who studied economics in college, and the only President who was once head of a labor union (Screen Actors Guild).

• There have been two sets of Presidents who were father and son: John Adams and John Quincy Adams, and George Bush and George W. Bush. Other Presidents who were related: William H. Harrison and Benjamin Harrison (grandfather and grandson); James Madison and Zachary Taylor (second cousins); and Theodore Roosevelt and Franklin D. Roosevelt (fifth cousins).

• Beginning in 1840, and in each consecutive 20-year presidential administration through 1960, the incumbent President has died in office. The "Twenty Year Curse" was supposedly cast upon the presidency at the hands of an unknown Indian chief.

• Seven Presidents have changed their names legally:

1. Ulysses Simpson Grant — changed from Hiram Ulysses Grant

2. Grover Cleveland — changed from Stephen Grover Cleveland

3. Woodrow Wilson — changed from Thomas Woodrow Wilson

4. Calvin Coolidge — changed from John Calvin Coolidge

5. Dwight David Eisenhower — changed from David Dwight Eisenhower

6. Gerald Rudolph Ford — changed from Leslie King, Jr. (changed when his mother remarried and his stepfather legally adopted him)

7. William Jefferson Clinton — changed from William Jefferson Blythe (changed when his mother remarried and his stepfather legally adopted him).

Facts About the Presidents, Joseph Nathan Kane, (New York: Simon & Schuster [Pocket Books], 1968 [5th printing])

RESOURCES & ORGANIZATIONS

Find out who are your local, state and national leaders at:

http://www.statelocalgov.net/

Senators:
http://www.senate.gov/general/contact_information/senators_cfm.cfm

House of Representatives:
http://www.house.gov/representatives/

Cabinet:
http://www.whitehouse.gov/administration/cabinet

Judicial:
http://www.supremecourt.gov/about/members.aspx

Volunteer/Civic/Learning/Serving Organizations

American Bar Association
www.americanbar.org
The largest voluntary association in the world. ABA provides law school accreditation, continuing legal education, information about the law, programs to assist lawyers and judges in their work, and inititive to improve the legal system for the public.

AmeriCorps
www.americorps.gov
AmeriCorps supports a broad range of local programs that engage Americans in intensive service to meet critical community needs and develop leaders.

American Red Cross
www.redcross.org
The American Red Cross has been the nation's premier emergency response organization.

American Veterans (AMVETS)
www.amvets.org
AMVETS is one of America's foremost veterans service organizations that has a proud history of assisting veterans and sponsoring numerous programs to serve our country and its citizens.

American Enterprise Institute (AEI)
www.aei.org
AEI is a community of scholars and supporters committed to expanding liberty, increasing individual opportunity, and strengthening free enterprise. Its purpose is to serve leaders and the public through research and education on the most important issues

of the day in the areas of economics, culture, politics, foreign affairs, and national defense.

Boy Scouts of America
www.scouting.org
The Boy Scouts of America provides a program that builds character, trains in the responsibilities of participating citizenship, and develops personal fitness.

Civic Education Project
www.civiceducationproject.org
The Civic Education Project, an international non-profit organization, has promoted pluralism and international standards in social science education in countries striving to develop their civil society capacity.

Center for Civic Education
www.civiced.org
The mission of the Center for Civic Education is to promote an enlightened and responsible citizenry that is committed to democratic principles and actively engaged in the practice of democracy in the United States and other countries.

CIVNET
www.civnet.org
CIVNET is a worldwide online civic education community of civic educators, scholars, policymakers, civic-minded journalists, non-government organizations, and other individuals promoting civic education all over the world.

CCEL: Center For Civic Education & Leadership
www.ccel.asu.edu
The mission of CCEL is the enhancement of civics education in PK-12 schools as a way to promote democracy and freedom.

Civic Education Project
www.civiceducationproject.org
The Civic Education Project® (CEP), an international non-

profit organization, has supported grassroots efforts to promote pluralism and international standards in social science education in transitioning countries.

Conservative Political Action Conference (CPAC)
www.conservative.org/cpac
CPAC is a project of the American Conservative Union Foundation (ACUF) and the nation's largest annual gathering of conservatives. CPAC brings together all of the leading conservative organizations and speakers who impact conservative thought in the nation. CPAC has been the premiere event for any major elected official or public personality seeking to discuss issues of the day with conservatives and has become the place to find our nation's current and future

CRFC: Constitutional Rights Foundation Chicago
www.crfc.org
CRFC is a nonprofit and nonpartisan organization working with elementary and secondary schools to develop critical thinking skills, civic participation, and commitment to the rule of law among young people.

CRF: Constitutional Rights Foundation
www.crf-usa.org
CRF seeks to instill in the nation's youth a deeper understanding of citizenship and to educate young people to become active and responsible participants in our society.

DID: Deliberating in a Democracy
www.deliberating.org
DID is a major six year teacher-based initiative, designed to improve teaching and learning of democratic principles and the skills of civic deliberation, conducted by The Constitutional Rights Foundation Chicago (CRFC), The Constitutional Rights Foundation in Los Angeles (CRF) and Street Law, Inc.

Girl Scouts of America
www.girlscouts.org
Girl Scouts develops personal leadership abilities, building courage, confidence and character to make the world a better place.

Hands on Network
www.handsonnetwork.org
Hands on Network, the largest volunteer network in the nation, inspires, equips and mobilizes people to change lives through service.

Heritage Foundation
www.heritage.org
The Heritage Foundation is a research and educational institution whose mission is to formulate and promote conservative public policies based on the principles of free enterprise, limited government, individual freedom, traditional American values, and a strong national defense.

International Volunteer Programs Association
wwwvolunteerinternational.org
The International Volunteer Programs Association is an association of non-governmental organizations involved in international volunteer work and internship exchanges.

International Fellowship of Christians & Jews (IFCJ)
www.ifcj.org
IFCJ was founded to promote understanding and cooperation between Christians and Jews.
The fellowship attempts to build broad support for Israel and other shared concerns. Poor, needy Jews around the world are assisted through programs of care and compassion.

Junior Achievement (JA)
www.ja.org
Junior Achievement is the world's largest organization dedicated to educating students about workforce readiness, entrepreneurship, financial literacy, and the value of contributing to their communities.

League of Women Voters (LWV)
www.lwv.org (vol)
The League of Women Voters is a nonpartisan, grassroots organization, working at the national, state and local levels to improve our systems of government and impact public policies through citizen education and advocacy.

Learn and Serve America
www.learnandserve.gov
Learn and Serve America supports and encourages service-learning throughout the United States, and enables over one million students to make meaningful contributions to their community while building their academic and civic skills. By engaging our nation's young people in service-learning, Learn and Serve America instills an ethic of lifelong community service.

Michigan Center for Civic Education
www.miciviced.org
The Center's mission is to promote and support the development of responsible citizens through study of civics, government and law in elementary and secondary schools.

NACE: National Alliance for Civic Education
www.cived.net
NACE is a combined effort of diverse groups and individuals helping citizens across the country better understand the significance of effective civic education for a well-functioning democracy.

National Literacy Coalition (NLC)
www.nationalliteracycoalition.org
The NLC provides training, ongoing support, and technical assistance to schools committed to a singular vision – all children can learn to read and write.

National Rifle Association (NRA)
www.nra.org
The NRA has been the premier firearms education organization in

the world. It is widely recognized today as a major political force and as America's foremost defender of Second Amendment rights.

National Service-Learning Clearinghouse
www.servicelearning.org
Service-Learning is a teaching and learning strategy that integrates meaningful community service with instruction and reflection to enrich the learning experience, teach civic responsibility, and strengthen communities.

National Youth Leadership Council
www.nylc.org
The mission of the National Youth Leadership Council is to create a more just, sustainable, and peaceful world with young people, their schools, and their communities through service-learning.

Peace Corps
www.peacecorps.gov
Peace Corps volunteers have served our country in the cause of peace by living and working in 139 developing countries.

Points of Light Institute
www.pointsoflight.org
Points of Light Institute strives to advance innovative civic strategies to shape national policy, to achieve impact through service and to build an engaged citizenry.

Service-Learning Partnership
www.service-learningpartnership.org
The Service-Learning Partnership is a national network of members dedicated to advancing service-learning as a core part of every young person's education.

Salvation Army
www.salvationarmyusa.org
The Salvation Army cooperates with all denominations to meet the needs of the community in the name of Jesus Christ without discrimination.

TCI: Teachers' Curriculum Institute
www.teachtci.com
TCI is a K – 12 social studies publisher with a mission of helping social studies educators engage all learners in the diverse classroom.

The Federalist Society
www.fed-soc.org
The Federalist Society for Law and Public Policy Studies is a group of conservatives and libertarians dedicated to reforming the current legal order. This organization is committed to the principles that the state exists to preserve freedom, the separation of governmental powers is central to our Constitution, and it is emphatically the province and duty of the judiciary to say what the law is, not what it should be. Overall, the Society's efforts are improving our present and future leaders' understanding of the principles underlying American law.

The Cato Institute
www.cato.org
The Cato Institute is a public policy research organization. Its mission is to increase the understanding of public policies based on the principles of limited government, free markets, individual liberty, and peace.

The Veterans Speakers Forum
pr.group@juno.com
How to educate students in the schools of Palm Beach County, Fl. About our War Hero's Honoring Those Who Served.

United Way
www.liveunited.org
United Way is a leadership and support organization that creates and supports innovative programs to generate sustained impact in local communities.

United We Serve
www.serve.gov
United We Serve is a nationwide service initiative that helps meet growing social needs resulting from the economic downturn.

VAVS: VA Voluntary Service
www.volunteer.va.gov
VAVS provides for our nation's veterans while they are cared for by VA health care facilities with end of life care programs, foster care, community-based volunteer programs, hospital wards, nursing homes, and veteran outreach centers.

Veterans of Foreign Wars (VFW)
www.vfw.org (civic)
The mission of the VFW is to: foster camaraderie among veterans of overseas conflicts; to serve our veterans, the military, and our communities; to advocate on behalf of all veterans.

Volunteers of America
www.voa.org
Volunteers of America, through thousands of human service programs, has supported and empowered America's most vulnerable groups.

VolunteerMatch
www.volunteermatch.org
VolunteerMatch is an organization offering a variety of online services to support a community of nonprofit, volunteer and business leaders committed to civic engagement.

We The People
www.wethepeople.gov
We the People is a National Endowment For The Humanities program designed to encourage / enhance the teaching, study, understanding of American history, culture and democratic principles.

We the People: The Citizen and the Constitution
http://new.civiced.org/programs/wtp
We the People is a curricular program offered at the upper elementary, middle, and high school levels that promotes civic competence and responsibility among the nation's students. The design of

the instructional program, including its innovative culminating activity in the form of a simulated congressional hearing, makes the program successful with both teachers and students. We the People is conducted by the Center for Civic Education with the assistance of a national network of state and congressional district coordinators in every state. The program enjoys the active participation of members of Congress, as well as support from educational, professional, business, and community organizations across the nation. Since its inception in 1987, more than 30 million students and 90,000 educators have participated in this innovative course of study.

We the People: Project Citizen
http://new.civiced.org/programs/project-citizen
Project Citizen is an active-learning curricular program for middle, secondary, and post-secondary students, youth organizations, and adult groups that promotes competent and responsible participation in local and state government. The program helps participants learn how to monitor and influence public policy. In the process, they develop support for democratic values and principles, tolerance, and feelings of political efficacy. Project Citizen is administered by the Center for Civic Education with the assistance of a national network of state and congressional district coordinators in every state and is conducted with the assistance of the National Conference of State Legislatures.

YLI: Youth Leadership Initiative
www.youthleadership.net
YLI, a program of the University of Virginia Center for Politics, develops free education resources designed to assist civics teachers and encourage students to participate in the political process.

Interactive

Civics Online
www.civics-online.org
Civics Online is a collaborative internet effort providing materials and resources to enhance current approaches to teaching civics in the classroom.

iCivics
www.icivics.org
iCivics (formerly Our Courts) is a web-based education project designed to teach students civics and inspire them to be active participants in our democracy. iCivics is the vision of Justice Sandra Day O'Connor, who is concerned that students are not getting the information and tools they need for civic participation and that civics teachers need better materials and support.

Annenberg Foundation Trust At Sunnylands
www.sunnylandstrust.org
Sunnylands Trust attempts to improve civics education and understanding of democratic institutions. In furtherance of that mission, the Trust creates and distributes print, online and video materials on the Constitution to provide schools and institutions with high-quality programs for use around Constitution Day in September and beyond.

Annenberg Classroom
www.annenbergclassroom.org
This website offers high school students civics news, student discussion, outstanding multimedia on the Constitution, or the engaging connection among all three.

Additional Resources

AAC&U: American Association of Colleges and Universities
www.aacu.org

AACTE: American Association of Colleges for Teacher Education
www.aacte.org

AASA: American Association of School Administrators
www.aasa.org

ABA: American Bar Association Division for Public Education
www.americanbar.org/groups/public_education.html

American Enterprise Institute
www.aei.org

American Federation of Teachers
www.aft.org
ASCD: Association for Supervision and Curriculum Development
www.ascd.org

Bill of Rights Institute
www.billofrightsinstitute.org

CIRCLE: Center for Information & Research on Civic Learning & Engagement
www.civicyouth.org

CSAE: Center for the Study of the American Electorate
www.american.edu/spa/cdem/csae.cfm

Cesar Chavez School for Public Policy
www.chavezschools.org

CEP: Character Education Partnership
www.character.org

City Year
www.cityyear.org

Close-Up Foundation
www.closeup.org

Coalition for Community Schools
www.communityschools.org

CED: Committee for Economic Development
www.ced.org

Corporation for National & Community Service
www.nationalservice.gov

CCSSO: Council of Chief State School Officers
www.ccsso.org

Earth Force, Inc.
www.earthforce.org

Forum for Education and Democracy
www.forumforeducation.org

FCL: Future Civic Leaders
www.futurecivicleaders.org

First Amendment Center
www.firstamendmentcenter.org

Generation Citizen
www.generationcitizen.org

ICP: Innovations in Civic Participation
www.icicp.org

JSA: Junior Statesmen Foundation
www.jsa.org

Kid's Voting U.S.A
www.kidsvoting.org

Lou Frey Institute for Politics and Government, Florida Joint Center for Citizenship
www.loufrey.orgprograms/floridaJointCenter.php

Mikva Challenge
www.mikvachallenge.org

NASSP: National Association of Secondary School Principals
www.nassp.org

NASBE: National Association of State Boards of Education
www.nasbe.org
National Catholic Educational Association
www.ncea.org

NCLC: National Center for Learning & Citizenship, Education Commission of the States
www.ecs.orghtml/projectsPartners/clc/clc_main.htm

NCOC: National Conference on Citizenship
www.ncoc.net

NCSL: National Conference of State Legislatures
www.ncsl.org

NCSS: National Council for the Social Studies
www.socialstudies.org

National Constitution Center
www.constitutioncenter.org

National Education Association
www.nea.org/

National Education Knowledge Industry Association
www.nekia.org

NHD: National History Day
www.nhd.org

NSBA: National School Boards Association
www.nsba.org

CCP: Netter Center for Community Partnerships, University of Pennsylvania
www.upenn.edu/ccp

P21: Partnership for 21st Century Skills
www.p21.org

PEN: Public Education Network
www.publiceducation.org

RMC Research, Inc.
www.rmcres.com

Rural School and Community Trust
www.ruraledu.org

Street Law Inc.
www.streetlaw.org

SEANET: State Education Agencies Service Learning Provider Network
www.seanetonline.org

The Forum for Youth Investment
www.forumfyi.org

Help us with our next edition of

CITIZENSHIP:
WHAT EVERY AMERICAN
NEEDS TO KNOW

Send additional information:

- **Resources/Organizations**
- **Inspirational Stories: People Making a Difference**
- **Endorsements/Comments about the book**

Send to: info@stargroupinternational.com

Visit us: www.stargroupinternational.com

StarGroup International

1194 Old Dixie Highway, Suite 201
West Palm Beach, Florida 33403

561-547-0667

Coming Soon

100 TOP AMERICAN COMPANIES
STARTED BY IMMIGRANTS